GROUND ZERO™

Starting All Over Again . . . with God

by Ron Cook
with Dee Kimbrell and Tom Hicks

WORD PUBLISHING
NASHVILLE
A Thomas Nelson Company

The Ground Zero™/MindFast™ Series is a series of printed publications, audio and video cassette tapes, and educational workshops, seminars, and retreats for those individuals seeking spiritual awareness and renewal.

MindFast™ and Ground Zero™ are trademarks of Quarterback Legends, Inc. and Ground Zero.

Scripture quotations in this book are from the New American Standard Bible (NASB), © 1960, 1977 by the Lockman Foundation.

Library of Congress Cataloging-in-Publication Data

Cook, Ron, 1949–
    Ground zero : starting all over again—with God / by Ron Cook : with Dee Kimbrell and Tom Hicks.
       p. cm.
    ISBN 0-8499-3724-8
    1. Christian life. I. Kimbrell, Dee, 1959– . II. Hicks, Tom, 1954– . III. Title.
    BV4501.2.C6733 1999
    248.8'4—dc21   99-21289
                                            CIP

Printed in the United States of America

9 0 1 2 3 4 BVG 9 8 7 6 5 4 3 2 1

Those who really know *you,* God, *will* trust *in* You, *for You have* never *forsaken those who seek* You.

KING DAVID, PSALM 9:10 (PARAPHRASE)

CONTENTS

FOREWORD

The life I lived as a college and NFL quarterback sounds like a fantasy to a lot of people. Even to me, my life has often seemed like a dream. I have no idea why I was given the talents and gifts that made it possible for me to play football and to play it well enough to succeed at a professional level. I can't tell you that I worked hard to learn how to throw the ball perfectly, or that I spent years studying and learning how to read defenses. My ability to play football came very naturally. And I have spent a considerable amount of time wondering about where all that comes from.

Today my three daughters are the love of my life. I think it is my relationship with the girls that sometimes causes me to find myself thinking about God. A parent/child relationship can't help but put thoughts about God in your mind, because such wonderful gifts as our children must come from a generous Giver. For reasons like that, I've always known that God is there. I've heard him called a lot of names, but for me, when it comes to God, there have always been more questions than answers.

When I met Ron Cook through Legends Management Group, I found out that he was the son of a preacher. But after hearing his references to God I became interested in his relationship with his God. So I asked him, "What do you think about the Big Guy?" I think that question, coming from me, jump-started Ronnie into sharing his relationship, starting at ground zero.

Even though Ron was surprised by the question, we discussed the "Big Guy" for several hours, and he made things as clear as he could. Then, in the months that followed that conversation, he did a lot more thinking. One question was stuck in his mind: "How can I find a way to explain God to people like Stabler, who have no church background, no spiritual language, and no interest in organized religion?" Ron spent the next three-and-a-half years looking for ways to answer that question. He read; he interviewed people; he reconsidered everything he'd ever been taught. And the book you are now holding in your hands is the result of his efforts.

This book has urged me to think—to think and to thank. To think about the how and the why. *Ground Zero*™ has encouraged me to assess my own relationship with God and to look at the things I love the most. Quarterbacks love game plans, and *Ground Zero*'s plan has this old quarterback calling plays again, trying to win a different game.

KEN STABLER
MOBILE, ALABAMA, 1999

BUSINESS REPLY MAIL

FIRST-CLASS MAIL   PERMIT NO. 104   WARMINSTER PA

POSTAGE WILL BE PAID BY ADDRESSEE

POWER FOR LIVING
PO BOX 5021
WARMINSTER PA 18974-9943

Please let us help you . . .

Check the box which applies to you:

☐ After reading this book, I have now prayed to invite Jesus Christ into my life.

☐ I am still uncertain about how to have a personal relationship with Jesus Christ.

If you checked either box above, we would like to send you a free copy of the *New Testament with Psalms and Proverbs.* Then we will also send you a free copy of *Steps to Christian Maturity,* a practical guide which will help you draw the most power for living from the Bible.

To receive these two books, simply print your name and address in the space provided below. No contributions will be solicited or accepted. These two books are yours absolutely free. Please allow four to six weeks for delivery.

PRINT NAME _____

ADDRESS _____

CITY_____STATE _____ZIP_____

Comments welcome. We sincerely regret that personal responses are not possible:

_____

_____

_____

_____

BEFORE WE BEGIN

When old Aristotle answered the question, "What is a friend?" he replied, "A single soul dwelling in two bodies." Actually, for Dee Kimbrell, Tom Hicks, and myself friendship dwells in three bodies. God has a unique way of bringing and bonding together the most unusual people at the strangest times for a common purpose more noble than anyone might have suspected.

So it is that we find ourselves sitting on my breezeway, three close friends gathered together to take a God-given idea and try to put it into words. There I am, a preacher's son who has spent his entire life promoting people and merchandise, writing a book about God. Next to me is an ex-hippie turned recycling entrepreneur, and beside him sits a beautiful, artistic mom who has a gift for teaching children about God through nature. I do not understand how we were brought together, but I do know why and by Whom.

For most people, the phrase "back to ground zero" is a fairly common expression. It means starting again with nothing. It usually has something to do with stripping away, with back to basics, with eliminating nonessentials. But for us, Ground Zero has a deeply spiritual and inspired meaning. When we speak of Ground Zero, we're talking about starting all over again with God. For us—and for the purposes of this book—it means getting rid of preconceived ideas, other people's opinions, and irrelevant religious images and discovering God one-on-one. By the time Ground Zero is reached, it also means a promising new beginning. And we are determined to find a way to communicate Ground Zero, and all it offers, to those who want to know who God really is.

My mind flashes away from the breezeway, back to another time and place—a hurried morning some years ago. My career involves the professional management and promotion of celebrities and former NFL quarterbacks. That morning I was flying to California with one of them—Kenny Stabler—for a promotional appearance. The overhead light had indicated that it was okay for us to loosen our seat belts, but the pilot was oblivious to what the next few minutes would bring. I was about to receive a jolt that would change my life forever.

Just as we were reaching the tops of the clouds, Kenny turned to me and asked very thoughtfully, "So, tell me what you think about the Big Guy."

Totally caught off guard, I more or less stammered, "The 'Big Guy'? Do you mean . . . God?"

"Yeah," he replied, nodding, "the Big Guy. I can tell

you have a different kind of relationship with Him. I want you to tell me about Him."

Fortunately for me, at about that time the flight attendant arrived at our seats and began taking Kenny's order for the in-flight meal. I looked out the window and began fighting back the tears. It was no secret that Kenny had a colorful reputation. I silently appealed to God: *You want* me *to tell Kenny Stabler about* You? *Kenny, "The Snake," Stabler, Bad Boy of the NFL? Who would have thought that he would even want to know about You?*

The stewardess interrupted my thoughts with a request for my order. I turned to Kenny when she had moved to the next row and I stalled, "So what do *you* think about Him?"

"I'm not sure what I think about Him," he began, "but I don't think He likes me very much. I think He frowns at me, *a lot.*" He pinched the skin between his eyes with his thumb and forefinger. "In fact, I think I am the one that put that big wrinkle right between His eyes."

We both chuckled at the image Kenny had painted with his words. It didn't take long for me to realize that he had been thinking long and hard about God, and the next few minutes turned very serious. The entire scope of what I thought about people "looking for God" was about to change. Kenny and I shared our "growing up" stories and a picture unfolded of a young, gifted athlete raised in a small southern Alabama town. His family didn't attend a church regularly, and no one had ever really talked to him about God.

His extraordinary skills in baseball and football were noticed as early as junior high school by legendary coach Paul "Bear" Bryant. After four championship seasons at the University of Alabama, Kenny was chosen in the second round of the 1968 draft and, as quarterback, took the Oakland Raiders to several division titles and eventually a victory in Super Bowl XI.

In all those years he hadn't exactly been in the frame of mind to think of needing "something more." After all, he was an All-Pro quarterback in the NFL. Everyone wanted to be his friend; he seemed to get whatever he wanted even before he asked. For Ken Stabler, life was one big party. He had it all. Who needed God?

But lately, he had begun wondering if there wasn't something to this "God stuff." It wasn't about the angry men he saw on TV who were pointing and shouting things about the end of time or the bad-hair preachers who held their weekly "beg-a-thons." It wasn't about the folks who were in the church pew every Sunday but didn't look any happier than he felt. It was about something much more personal than that—he knew that there was an emptiness within him that kept bringing his thoughts back to God.

I thought of my own childhood filled with Vacation Bible Schools, Christian youth groups, and Sunday afternoon dinners on the church grounds. Everyone in my family got up on Sunday morning and went to church. There was never a question, no decision to make. That was just how we did things. God and church (not necessarily in that order) were interwoven into the fabric of our family. It was as much a part of who we were as the fact that our last name was Cook.

How could I have been so blind? I never thought that in this country there might be people who could live their whole lives without knowing about God. And yet here, sitting beside me, was a famous, worldly-wise, middle-aged man who was as innocent to all the trappings of religion as a three-year-old child. Again, I blinked back the tears.

"You're different from others that I've heard talk about God." Kenny was not chuckling now, but looking at me very intently. "He seems very real to you. How did that happen?"

I grinned, both at God and to myself. Yes, God is very real to me. But that has not always been the case. I began to tell Kenny of my own quest to make God personally real. Although I had been brought up to know all *about* God, I had never really gotten to *know* Him until just a few years before. Back then, I was the owner of a successful wholesale jewelry business with a very elite clientele. Life was good. Then suddenly, the business fell apart. As you might guess, most of the friends disappeared as quickly as the cash.

After spending day after day confronting collection agencies and seeing the faces of disappointed acquaintances, I found myself lying facedown on my living room floor in the middle of the night asking some very tough questions. To my distress, I quickly realized that all of the "right" answers sounded extremely hollow in my ears. I had nothing to offer God, nothing to bargain with, so this is what I said to Him:

"I don't know what I believe anymore. I am tired of playing the church game and feeling empty. I don't know if You really do talk to people. I do know that I don't have anything to give to You except my time. But I will promise You this: I will spend time every day with You, trying to listen to what You have to tell me. And I won't take anyone else's opinion if You'll just teach me Yourself."

Every morning I began to get up before everyone else in the house and started what I refer to as my "Thinkin' and Thankin' Time." I began to think of all the many things that He had given to me: family, friends, wife, healthy children, and suddenly I had spent hours "thinking and thanking." I could not begin to think all of those things without being filled to the brim with gratitude to the One who provided them. When I looked at the birds outside my window, I was reminded that if He provides for them, He will surely provide for me. This new awareness of God's goodness filled me with a sense of security that followed me around all day long.

Even now, nine years later, I am still keeping my "appointment" with God early every morning, and I still do my "Thinkin' and Thankin' Time." My time includes some reading and study, but mostly I make it a point to just be still and allow God to exchange thoughts with me. I tried to explain all this to Ken Stabler. I hope he understood.

That plane ride was just an ordinary flight with bad food and little legroom, but it changed my entire life. It stirred in me a passion to reach men and women like Kenny, to tell them what a loving God we have. The

God I know is not an angry old man with, as Kenny put it, "a big wrinkle in His forehead" from frowning so much. The God I know won't zap you for making a mistake. He is a loving God with His hand outstretched, eager to walk with you on the journey of a lifetime.

I know this because it has been my experience. It has been Dee's and Tom's experience. We've all three been to Ground Zero, and we want it to be your experience too.

After I initially shared my concerns and my vision with Tom and Dee, we spent three and a half years talking with hundreds of people of every race, creed, religion, and occupation about who they are, who God is, and what they can do with God empowering them. Now, at last, the time has come for my two friends and me to put into words what we have learned.

Everyone wants to be loved by God and to love God. Unfortunately, most people just don't know where to start or, worse, they are afraid to start. Religion can sometimes seem so complicated and overwhelming. Religious people can seem remote and unaware. But we don't want to talk about religion— that is the last thing on our minds. We simply want to present a clear, simple message of who God is and what He means to us, a message that anyone and everyone can understand.

Have you longed to know God intimately but haven't known where to begin? Are you ready to begin your own journey toward Ground Zero where you can actually meet God? In the pages that follow, we hope you'll discover what three friends—Dee, Tom, and I—have come to understand more certainly than anything else we know. Each of us wants nothing more than to share with you the best news you'll ever hear:

- God designed you, made you, and loves you.
- God wishes only good things for you and is prepared to open your eyes and ears to the beauty of His wonderful creation so you can start really loving Him back.
- God and you together are special and unique, and there's no limit to what you and He can accomplish together!

Chapter One

QUESTIONS FOR SEEKERS

Happiness is having your heart set on the quest.
—PSALM 84:5 (PARAPHRASE)

What is the toughest question you've ever faced? It may have been about life and death. It may have been about good and evil. It may have been just one or two words: Why? Why me? There are several other candidates for the toughest question of all:

> *Why are we here?*
> *Is there a personal God out there?*
> *What is the meaning of life?*

The tougher the questions, the farther we have to reach for answers. And if you're like a lot of busy people, most days you'd just as soon avoid the questions and worry about the answers later—much later. Or you might shrug your shoulders and reply with a smile, "Who knows? Life is a journey . . ."

Of course life-as-a-journey is a familiar cliché. In fact it's more than that: it's a metaphor that comes pretty close to the truth. But when you think of life as a journey, you're immediately faced with more questions than ever. That's because so much of life's journey is shrouded in mystery.

You never really know what a hairpin turn or a steep grade will reveal on the other side. And you probably face each day with any number of emotions—fear, sorrow, anxiety, hope, or joy. Come morning, you either welcome the dawn with a delightful sense of anticipation, or you growl at the alarm clock and roll over for another five minutes' sleep. In any case, you eventually have to get up, get dressed, and start down the road again—a road that leads to unknown opportunities, unplanned encounters, and unforeseen events.

Achievers, Dreamers, and Seekers

No matter what each new day may offer, you are the one who has to make sense of it. That means you have to make sense of yourself. And that means more questions:

> *Who are you?*
> *How well do you know yourself?*
> *What are you really like?*

Are you an achiever? If so, you probably have a fairly well-defined vision of what you'd like to see happen in your future. With that in mind, you try to keep your daily life focused on your long-term goal. Your special vision for your life may involve romance, family, financial security, or personal achievement. In order to see that vision become reality, you try to maintain some control over your activities so you will continue moving in the right direction. This means that you are always sifting through your opportunities, encounters, and events, treasuring some and discarding others. You use life's journey as a means to an end.

Are you a dreamer? If so, you are probably convinced that your journey itself is all that matters. Since you intend simply to enjoy the journey for its own sake, you may not be particularly concerned with goals. More likely, your attention is given to the people you meet, to the pursuit of pleasure, and to the avoidance of pain. For you, the journey is the destination. You use life's journey as an experience.

Whether you are an achiever or a dreamer, whether you know who you are or aren't so sure, whether you are reluctant or exuberant, you are most certainly on the road to *somewhere*. Like everyone else on earth, you are moving along life's journey one step at a time. Depending on your mood, your present circumstances, or your personal point of view, you may identify yourself as a survivor or an adventurer, a victim or a victor, a free spirit or a serious thinker. At some point along the way, every person is probably all of these and more.

No matter how free-spirited you are, for example, you are bound to have had some serious thoughts along the way; just about everybody does. By now, you've probably asked yourself all the tough questions, and a few more besides:

Is there any reason for my journey?
Can anyone see where I am headed?
Does Somebody somewhere have plans
   for my future?

Maybe you believe in God, but you don't feel as if you know God very well. Maybe you used to believe, but you were never too sure who or what it was you believed in. Maybe you've never been able to trust in something you can't see or feel or touch. If you're like a lot of people I've talked to, you would love nothing better than to know more of God, to increase your faith, and to experience something beyond yourself. But when you get to the point of doing something about it, you don't know what to do.

Seekers see life as a journey, too, but they believe that the journey is, in fact, a spiritual quest. You might say that they are both dreamers and achievers, because they are pursuing a goal as well as living the journey for its own sake. For them, there is a destination at the end of the journey, a destination that extends beyond the earthly and into the eternal. An ultimate encounter with God is the seeker's quest, while paradoxically, God is present throughout the journey.

A SEEKER'S MINDFAST

Are you a seeker? Would you like to be? If you are longing to take a journey with God and toward God, you will first need a change of mind, a new way of thinking. Much of this book is devoted to something I call a

"MindFast™." This MindFast initially was designed to take place over a twenty-eight-day period, but the time spent in the process is quite irrelevant. You can take a year or a month, or you may wish to do it all in one weekend. You may wish to complete all three portions of each day's journal at the same time, or you may only want to do one portion each day. There's no magic formula; the schedule is entirely up to you.

MindFast simply means that while you are beginning to explore who God is and who you are, you'll need to slow your mind down and really start to understand that there is no way to communicate with God except through your thoughts. As you work through the MindFast, you will be deliberately spending quiet time with God. You will be saying to God, "I'm processing many of the questions I have about You, about who You are, and about my life. *I need Your assistance.*" Be assured that God will be there to help you.

Throughout history, men and women in search of closer communion with God have gone to solitary places for prayer and contemplation. They have voluntarily removed themselves from the crowds, the demands, the distractions, and the pressures they've faced each day and have chosen to be alone with God. In today's high-speed, stressful world, occasional periods of isolation may be even more important for you and me than they were for the people of old. Now and then, that means no cell phone, no beeper, no computer, no radio, no TV. It means you, the creation, and the Creator. Period.

As you begin your journey and move into the

MindFast, there are some points I'd like for you to contemplate along the way.

First, can you acknowledge that *God is in everything?* God is everywhere, all-knowing, and all-powerful. God is life and light and love. God is Spirit. God is always present, even in the midst of life's most puzzling and painful circumstances. God created all things, and all creation exists in God. Earnestly seek, and your Creator will reveal to you ever so gently, ever so wonderfully, that God really is in everything, and apart from God nothing can exist.

Second, *can you relax and live today?* Have you ever noticed how difficult it is to relax? If we believe that God is in everything and have come to recognize God's presence around and within us, then we can learn, over a period of time, to relax and trust. God is in control and is involved in everything—what has happened, what is happening, and what will happen in the future. Most of us don't relax because we are afraid, and we are afraid because we don't really believe in God's power and goodness. But we are wrong: God is all powerful and God is all good. Meanwhile, yesterday is gone, tomorrow is unknown, today is all we have, and the "present" really is a gift. We need to relax, let go of worries, fears, doubts, and hurts and live right here, right now.

Finally, *can you learn simply to listen and receive?* God never stops communicating with us. God is never silent and is forever revealing Himself all around us in countless ways. The problem is that we are not listening. God never stops giving, but we are not always open to receive all that is available to us.

Beginning Your Quest

Since the beginning of time, all humankind has participated in a search for the meaning of life. Your Creator has placed within you a longing for a relationship with Him. You may have ignored the longing or intended to pursue it at another time. Your search may have been misguided. Or you may have left the path toward God and headed down a detour, trying to fill your longing for God with something tangible but terribly inadequate. Whatever happened, you are still feeling empty, still wanting something—Someone—that you cannot seem to find.

You may never have darkened the door of a church in your life, with the possible exception of weddings, funerals, and Christmas pageants. Perhaps you prefer to spend your Sunday mornings with a Bloody Mary and the newspaper. Your idea of a beautiful cathedral may be the forest, the beach, or even the golf course. Your primary acknowledgment of God's existence might be reflected in the colorful language of your angry outbursts.

Or your story may be entirely different. You may have spent much of your life going to church. You may have attended faithfully, said the right words, prayed the right prayers, and tried to be "good." If yours was a rule-keeping church, you kept up with whatever standards you could, failing at times and therefore facing people's not-so-loving judgment. If yours was a congregation that believed in putting everybody to work in the church, you may have gladly participated, teaching classes, driving buses, spending hours volunteering for projects, perhaps to the point of burnout. If yours was a church that studied Scripture, you may have thrown yourself wholeheartedly into knowing about doctrine, about history, about ancient languages, and maybe even about God. But did you ever really get to know God? Or was the "god" you met smaller than the One you wanted to believe in?

One man I interviewed was from a small town in the South. He was a deep thinker, the kind of guy who asks all the hard questions. Our dialogue was difficult because he questioned and challenged everything I said. At first I couldn't understand his argumentative attitude, but then he explained.

He was white and his best friend was black, a fine athlete he'd played football with since high school. He and his friend had always talked about God. Some years before our conversation, he had taken his friend with him to his small church, and the congregation refused to allow his friend to become a member of their church because of his color.

It was clear that this man had a deep, profound love for God and a desire to know God in an intimate and personal way. But he told me, "I believe in God, but the God they talk about in church is not the God that I know. I believe there are no limits, no bounds, no qualifications that you must follow in terms of race, color, or creed to define whether God loves you or not."

Then there was the prostitute I talked to in Las Vegas. Although she quickly discovered that I wasn't interested in her "escort" service, she was willing to answer my questions about the "Big Guy." I discovered that this woman had a lively interest in God but was confused by religion. She very quickly let me know that she wanted to know God and she believed God was there. But she didn't see how He could love her because of what she did for a living. She knew very well that she wouldn't get to know Him in church because she was convinced the church people wouldn't even let her through the door. "I don't like church, anyway," she said with a defensive grin.

You may have your own story about church, about how you failed to meet God there, about how people drove you away from your quest to meet God. Whatever happened to you in church, or in the process of being religious, may have kept you from getting to know God personally. Or you may have had no contact with church at all, having simply turned away from ideas about God until "later." That was then. What about now?

Would you like to know God today?

In this book you will begin your MindFast—the very first steps on your journey with God, toward God, and perhaps back to God. You aren't going to need much baggage as you move along, so I suggest you leave behind some of your past ideas and preconceived notions. For example, you may have a mental picture of God—the "Old Man Upstairs," the "Big Guy," or maybe George Burns—that comes to mind when you try to think about or talk to God. Set that picture aside for now, because I can assure you that your image of God is far too small.

Or, depending on your background, your idea of God could be quite the opposite. You may imagine God to be a vast, impersonal force or energy flow that enlivens the universe but does not concern itself with the daily, personal journey of ordinary people like you. Set that idea aside too.

In fact, for now don't worry about anything you've been taught about God at all. Instead, make up your mind to allow God to communicate with you without seeking anyone else's interpretation. Let God speak with you directly.

I suggest that you have a private conversation with God. Speak openly, honestly, and bluntly. Express any fear, uncertainty, or emotion that you are feeling. Tell Him you don't know what to expect. Tell Him if you are confused or afraid. Remember, I had a similar conversation with God on my living room floor nine years ago. I can assure you of one thing: God will teach, guide, and protect a sincere, inquiring heart and mind on a personal quest to know Him. God does not trick or pull the rug out from under an earnest seeker. For nine wonderful years of morning quiet time, He has never left me alone or out in the cold—never. So relax, and trust that God can handle your smallest and biggest concerns. (After all, He already knows everything you are thinking and feeling anyway.)

In the next twenty-eight days, you will find yourself on a stunning panoramic tour of the wonders of God, wonders that are revealed through the ever-changing kaleidoscope of creation and human life. You will learn to appreciate silence and not to fear it. You will set aside your fears and begin to know serenity and peace. And you will begin to discover the answers to the three most important questions of all:

> *Who is God?*
> *Who am I?*
> *Who are God and I together?*

Before long, this early part of your journey will be over, and you'll arrive at base camp—Ground Zero. At that point you won't be finished at all. In fact, your journey will only have just begun. But you will have a far better understanding of your life's path, your Guide, and your destination. You will have begun to affirm and live out the truth of God's ancient promise to all true seekers:

> *"For I know the plans I have for you," declares the* LORD, *"plans to prosper you and not to harm you, plans to give you hope and a future. Then you will call upon Me and come and pray to Me, and I will listen to you. You will seek Me and find Me when you search for Me with all your heart."* (Jeremiah 29:11–13)

Chapter Two

WHO IS GOD?

Earth, with her thousand voices, praises God.
—SAMUEL TAYLOR COLERIDGE

I grew up in a small town in east Tennessee, a town like many in the Appalachians, nestled between ridges of green mountains. Huge stone outcroppings appeared gray on misty mornings and glittered like silver on bright sunny afternoons.

In the middle of our town was Coal Creek, named no doubt for the industry that provided a livelihood for my grandfather and others like him. They were Scottish and Irish working men who very rarely saw the light of day and whose hands bore the color of the coal that heated their homes and put food on their tables.

The creek flowed right past our home, a two-story, wood-frame house. Our hedge enclosed a garden filled with rose bushes, irises, forsythias, and, behind the coal house, sweet mountain grapes. The front door adjoined a large porch with columns and a wide railing. As with most houses, a swing that could accommodate two adults or four children was positioned to face the two-lane road that separated our property from the creek bank.

On hot summer nights, neighbors and even passersby would stop and find a comfortable seat to just "jaw." My mother would serve the best lemonade in the world or sometimes the kids would be sent to Disney's Market for cokes.

Some folks would put peanuts in their drinks. Others would take a sip and blow on the rim of the bottle's lip creating a tuba-like sound. The conversation would turn to who was sick, who had died, and basically any other tragedy that the town had experienced of late. Next, the gossip mongering would begin followed by the latest tales of humor generated by the town drunk, who rode an old Harley-Davidson through storefront windows, or the sexual escapades of a notorious preacher or an unrepentant town councilman.

Then, almost supernaturally, the conversation would turn to God. It would begin with small sprinklings of "Thanks," maybe for the good, sweet corn crop, the remission of a great-aunt's cancer, or for the black lung check arriving a few days earlier than usual. There was no mistaking that the handling of these daily blessings was not in the hands of men but solely in the hands of God. Every reference to God was prefaced with "Good." The Good Lord did good things. And stories with uncertain endings culminated with the classic conclusion: "It's all in the hands of the Good Lord."

We kids would usually finish our drinks and then

play hide-and-seek in the darkness early on, but we almost always ended up on the swing covered up in a blanket when the God-talk started. In fact, I assumed that God was sitting on that porch sipping a coke with us, nodding His head, and quietly saying, "You are welcome!" every time one of His tender mercies was expressed. He looked a little like that picture of Jesus that hung on the wall of my Sunday school classroom. I think it was those gentle eyes, but He also looked like one of us, simple countrypeople who loved each other, sins and all.

Even in those early days, I sensed God all around me and in me. It seemed to begin somewhere up in those mountains, and then the gentle spirit of God, moving like a cool evening breeze, would breathe upon my freckled face.

More than anything else, I felt that I belonged. I felt that this place and these people belonged to me. And I knew that God indeed may have been out there among those shining stars, but that He was also on the front porch with us, having a drink, sharing our stories with us.

That beautiful portrait of country life depicts one of Tom Hicks's earliest memories of God. Does that sound like the God you've heard about? Would it surprise you to discover that God can be that friendly, that approachable, that "down-home"?

From the time we are born until we die, every one of us is searching for the meaning of life. We all want to believe that we have a purpose on this planet. We long to be sure that what we do matters. We have a heartfelt hope that our existence is significant. When our search is carried to its logical conclusion, I think it's safe to say that we are all on a quest for God.

We have all been taught lots of different things about who God is. Well-meaning people have put some of the ideas in our heads, but some of the things we've heard may not be true. For one thing, when people talk about anything it usually comes out like the childhood game called "gossip"—by the time it gets to the end of the line it is a completely different story. Stories, ideas, or beliefs about God can be that way too. That's why we need to seek God for ourselves.

One of the big misconceptions is that God is a physical being—some sort of a big, superhuman person. In our interviews with people, we've learned that a surprising number of them think of God as an old man sitting on a throne. Depending on who gave them their ideas, this old man may be permanently scowling like Ken Stabler imagined, or doddering and grandfatherly. Does your conception of God look something like that? I can assure you that, whatever God is, He is not the "Old Man Upstairs."

Every one of us needs to question all our ideas about God, and I believe that God is big enough to handle our questions. In fact, I believe He wants us to ask questions. Until you actually *think* through for yourself what you believe about God, your ideas aren't really yours; they are your parents', your grandmother's, your teacher's, or somebody else's. When it comes to your knowing God, *your* experiences, encounters, and evidences are the only ones that matter.

So how can you find out about God? That's what you'll be exploring during your MindFast. You'll become aware of God around you, you'll become conscious of what He has given you, and you'll become sensitive to His endless, amazing creativity. Take time while you are driving, while you are walking, while you are sitting quietly to look around at the trees, at the sky, at the birds, at all the beautiful colors and shapes and textures, the sights and sounds and smells of life around you.

Our failure to notice the presence of God around us is similar to the predicament of a small child trying to get a parent's attention. The parent is talking to a friend or busy doing something else and doesn't even see or hear the child at their side, clamoring for attention. I believe God is like that with us. He is so intent on having a relationship with us that He keeps trying to get us to look His way. Everybody has a time when God speaks directly to them, "Listen to Me!" If we don't stop and pay attention, God's voice will get louder, because that's how much He loves us.

Some people have to "hit the wall," whatever that means for them, before they will wake up and realize there is another power greater than themselves. Only then will they depend on that power. But why wait to hit the wall? God wants you to know Him here and now, and He's trying to draw you to Himself with love and kindness. He'll eventually get your attention one way or another.

As Dee, Tom, and I share with you about who we believe God is, please don't misunderstand our intentions. We are not telling you what you ought to think. We're not telling you what you ought to experience. We aren't taking the role of being yet another "voice of authority." We simply want to share with you what we have learned during our own quest for God and through our compilation of responses from hundreds of people who answered our question, "What do you think about the 'Big Guy'?"

It's interesting—even though each person's experience is different, just about everybody we have talked to in our interviews has come to the same *personal* experience with God that we have. But as you read what we say about God, *please don't take our word for it.* What we want most of all is for you to discover for yourself who God is. We believe you'll find out that God is light, love, truth, spirit, breath, and peace. We believe you will come to see, as we have, that God is in everything. And we are absolutely sure that you will begin to realize that God loves you.

God Is Designer

How long has it been since you took the time to carefully examine the structure of a leaf? Or to watch a procession of storm clouds rumbling across the sky? Or to consider the exquisite miracle of a newborn baby? The more closely you examine the endless panorama of nature, the more intricate the design of every created thing becomes, and the more varied. Not only is every leaf a masterpiece of design, but, like people and snowflakes, no two leaves are exactly the same.

You might be a doctor or a microbiologist or an astronomer. Or you might be an ordinary person who just takes the time to think about the world around you. Either way, you know that there is nothing simple about the way nature works. To imagine all of creation coming into being without a Designer, with no thought or intention or purpose, is absurd. It makes no sense. The odds against such a random accident are beyond calculation.

Even more amazing than the complexity of each facet of creation is the big picture: everything God made is part of His perfect design. It all fits together, works together, complements itself, and sustains itself. The entire universe displays and confirms God's awesome design: planets, sun, moon, earth, seasons, weather cycles, plant life, animal life. And—we'll talk more about it in the next chapter—God's most intricate and personal design is *you!*

God Is Creator

Not only does everything around us have a remarkably intricate design, but everything has a purpose: the bird eats the ladybug that eats the aphids that feed on the leaves that absorb the carbon dioxide, and on and on it goes.

Everything God made began as a thought—a "God-thought." Somehow, God created material things from nothing but God-thoughts, making invisible thoughts into physical objects. And everything God created—and is still creating—is good. One part of creation is beyond our human grasp. Try as we might, we can't create *life*. Life is God's own unique gift to creation. All created things have God's pulse running through them; God put

Himself into everything that He created. By this I mean that the life that throbs through all things bears witness to the Creator God who *is* Life itself.

Humankind can misuse nature, but the things God made were created for us and they are wonderful. God is in everything: a tree, a dog, a star, an ocean. Of course, when I say that I don't mean that you should worship a tree or any other created thing. But if you study the tree and give some thought to it, you will be amazed by it and be blessed by its beauty, by its place in the landscape, by its changing colors, by its bark and roots and branches, by the fruit it bears, and by the shade it provides.

I interviewed a farmer from Nebraska who told me how important and personal God is to him. God was very real to this man because he saw God, day in and day out, on the farm and in the natural world around him. Over the years he had taken care to notice every phase of growth, from the planting of the crops to the harvest, and he saw God's hand in all of it.

This man did not go to church regularly, although he occasionally visited small country churches. But his relationship was not with a church. It was with God and it was intimately personal. This farmer believed strongly in prayer, and he talked to God, and he knew God answered him and provided for him and his family. He, along with many others I've spoken to, confirmed my conviction that we *can* meet God by observing nature.

This man was simply stunned by God's presence in the world and by watching the love of God revealed to him every day through nature. When he took the time to reflect upon the natural world without distractions, God reminded him that He is at work all the time. Like most of us, the farmer couldn't really explain the purpose of hurricanes, drought, earthquakes, and tornadoes—the aspects of nature that are hard for all of us to understand in terms of God. But things like that didn't confuse him at all, because he saw God as his personal provider and protector, as a constant and faithful friend. He didn't say so, but I know he knew God as a lover, as the One who loved him best.

GOD IS LOVER

The term "lover" is a problem for some people when it is applied to God. For them, the word *lover* depicts someone elusive or sexual or romantic. But when we use the word *lover* in terms of God, we're talking about intimacy. We're talking about a God with whom we can have a relationship more intimate than could be possible with anyone else. God knows you better than you know yourself. God loves you more than anyone can ever love you. And God wants, more than anything else, to have an intimate relationship with you.

Stop for a moment, and think about falling in love. Do you remember the overwhelming emotions? Do you recall the time you spent, the effort you put into it, the extra trouble you took? Well, think about this: God is in love with you! How will you respond? Can you imagine falling in love with your Creator?

Not only does God love you perfectly, but everything God made is an expression of His perfect love. Every person you know, every person in the world, every person God ever made is an expression of His love. Every person He made is of equal value in His eyes. There is no one on earth more important to God than you, there is no one God loves more, and there is no one with whom God is more interested in having a deep and intimate relationship than *you*.

The most amazing thing about God's love is that it is unconditional. You may have been told that before, but the truth is better than anything you've ever heard. Because everything you have ever wanted to believe about God's unconditional love is true. There is no one more worthy of His love than you. There is nothing you can do to make God love you more. There is nothing you can do to make God love you less. God's love is perfect love. His love for you, and for everyone else, does not and cannot change because of seasons or circumstances or thoughts or actions. God loves you perfectly. God *is* love!

GOD IS GIVER

During our three years of meeting together, of seeking God individually, and of talking to other people about God, Dee, Tom, and I have come to believe that God has already given us everything we need. That's a tough statement for some people to hear, but let me explain what I mean.

I don't want to give you the idea that if you'll just pray to God you will get a pink Cadillac or a million dollars or the romance of the century. What I mean is that, with God's help and because of God's generous provision, the human race has the resources to feed and clothe the whole world. But, unfortunately, because we humans are not always good stewards of what we've been given, some people in the world aren't fed and clothed. In effect, God has given everything to the person who is dying in Sudan or in some other famine-ravaged place on the other side of the world *because He has given humankind everything*. The problem of human suffering doesn't lie with God. The problem lies in what we humans do with God's provisions for the earth.

One of the most difficult questions that comes up when you are trying to understand "God as giver" is "If God is all good, why are hunger, suffering, pestilence, and other bad things in the world?" This brings to mind an interesting story.

Some businesspeople arrive at a restaurant known for its fantastic luncheon buffet. They become so immersed in their conversation that they lose track of time while they are waiting. But as they are talking, oblivious to what is going on around them, restaurant personnel have been preparing a massive buffet with salads, breads, cheeses, meats, vegetables, and desserts.

One guy with his back to the buffet suddenly interrupts the conversation and says, "Man! I wish they'd get the food out here! I'm starving!"

The buffet is prepared and waiting for them only a few feet away, yet they are starving to death. All they have to do is turn around and take whatever they want.

Humankind has been given everything, every opportunity, every physical and spiritual blessing, and there's enough for everyone. But a good, generous God has given the task of caring for others to each of us. You see, along with the other gifts that are built into us by our Designer, the human race is the only creation on earth to which God has given the ability to think, to reason, and to dream without limits. We are the only creation on earth to which God has given the ability to experience anything that we can imagine and pursue. Within that unique capability lies a corresponding responsibility; we are designed and created to love, to care for, and to give to one another.

None of us love perfectly or give perfectly. God is the only perfect and unconditional giver. Because of who God is, He continues to give us everything, even when we give Him nothing in return.

Awed Not Afraid

Designer, Creator, Lover, Giver—these are all aspects of God that we can experience for ourselves. Becoming aware of God's existence and presence is the first step toward discovering Him and starting a relationship with Him. Once you discover how awesome God is, then you quite naturally want to spend more time with Him.

An age-old proverb says, "The fear of the Lord is the beginning of wisdom." Now that bothers some people, because they think it means that God wants to see them trembling in their boots. But that's not what the phrase means. "The fear of the Lord" means a deep awe and wonder that comes from knowing God intimately. Being afraid of God is something we have to be taught.

One summer Tom Hicks and his family were in Switzerland at Schilthorn Mountain. At the top of the mountain is a restaurant that was featured in one of the James Bond films. If you step outside the restaurant, you can walk along the edge of the mountain, and the scenery is just breathtaking. From a vantage point about ten thousand meters high, you can see the snow-capped Alps and the beautiful green valleys below them. And the Hickses were there on a rare day—warm, cloudless, no fog.

The walking areas are not enclosed with handrails and fencing, and some guys were jumping off with hang gliders. Tom's little girl, who was five years old at the time, darted past the family and ran out in front to get a better look. There is loose gravel and a huge drop-off, and an adult feels a tingling sensation looking over the edge. But this little girl was walking along as if there were no danger, as if she were on a safe neighborhood sidewalk.

Tom's wife, Melanie, was feeling more nervous by the minute. "Madeleine!" she called out, "you've got to stay with us and hold our hands because it is a big drop-off and you could get hurt!"

Tom was curious about his daughter's calm state of mind, and he asked, "Madeleine, aren't you afraid you are going to fall?"

Madeleine looked at her dad and shook her head no.

"Why not?" Tom persisted.

The little girl pointed her finger toward the sky, smiled, and simply kept on walking.

The walk we are taking with God requires that kind

of trust. Trust is based on love. And love—perfect love, which comes from God—eliminates all fear. Children understand that God's love is safe and secure.

GOD'S MESSAGE TO YOU

A woman named Karen told us about her Ground Zero experience. She was standing by her kitchen window one day, thinking about God, and longing to know Him better. She found herself speaking to Him aloud, "God, I want to experience You. I want to feel Your presence in my life! Please, let me see You!"

Words spilled across Karen's mind, and she quickly wrote them down. This was God's answer to her, and we think it is His answer to us, and to you, and to every person who is on a quest for God.

It is not in one spectacular experience that you will come to know Me intimately. It is in living with Me every hour of every day.

You will see My face in all that is around you.

You will see Me in all of nature—the trees and sky and flowers, the sea, and the animals.

You will see Me in the faces of those who love you and whom you love.

You will see Me in the faces of all you meet and touch each day, for I am there.

You will hear Me speaking from everywhere. I am not limited; I speak in My written Word, in the writings of others, in the singing of birds, in the laughter of children.

Listen, for you cannot miss My voice. I will speak to you through the words of people. Their voices will bring you My messages.

I am in every circumstance, in every situation. I am everywhere, in everything, and I can use everyone, even if they don't recognize it.

You cannot miss Me if you but look and listen, for it is in your own eyes and in your own ears that you will see and hear Me.

It is in choosing to see the good in everything that happens to you, to take the blessing from each moment, each new day, each encounter with others.

It is in seeking Me, day after day, year after year, and finding Me always there, always waiting, always loving, always merciful, and always giving that you will learn to find the best in every person and situation and take from each the gifts that they bring.

You will experience Me and My presence when you can see Me in all things.

Chapter Three

WHO ARE YOU?

In the depth of winter, I finally learned that within me lay an invincible summer.

—ALBERT CAMUS

Gordon grew up in a rural community and he always had dreams of financial success. He worked hard, and by middle age he had achieved his ambition. One day while he was in Cincinnati on a business trip, he received a phone call from his mother and she told him that his father was very ill. His kidneys had failed and the doctor didn't expect him to live.

At dinner that evening and later in the quietness of his hotel room, Gordon remembered just how much he and his father were alike. It dawned on him that their similarity was partly responsible for their not being close. Maybe there was a fear that if they really got to know each other they might see some aspect of themselves that they wouldn't like. In any case, they had made the best of the father-son role but, once the rebellious teenage years arrived, they gradually went their separate ways.

The next day Gordon flew home and the following evening learned that his father had died. Gordon was stunned. He performed his nightly routine in a robot-like style and went to bed, but in the middle of the night he awoke, and he cried, and he cried, and he cried. He kept whispering over and over, "I really loved you, Dad."

As he drove to the funeral, somewhere along the four-hour stretch between the city where he lived and the rural community where he grew up, Gordon hit Ground Zero. He thinks it started when he began seeing the physical signs that he was going home: the look of the hills, the trees, the smells, the old black crows, the familiar lake. It continued at the funeral. There a preacher friend of his father's who had been present as the old man drew his last breath shared his dad's final utterance. The words hit Gordon like a sledgehammer. For as he was dying his dad had said, "I love God; I really love God."

Gordon realized that whatever physical similarities or resemblance he shared with his father, the one true bond that they had was that they both loved God. That would bind them together forever. The only sad thing was that his dad hadn't found out about God until he was dying. Gordon, on the other hand, because of his Ground Zero experience, encountered God in time to live the balance of his life walking with Him on his journey.

THE REAL YOU

Gordon was confronted with his "real" self because he saw his mirror image in the memory of his father. Up until that time, he had hidden away an important part of himself. I think everybody, to an extent, has a public persona, the face we put on when we cross some imaginary line and meet the world. We may be feeling our worst, but immediately there's a smile on our face when we see someone we know. Sometimes we are well aware of what we really feel and choose not to impose our moods on others. But if we don't know who we really are, our real self is hidden from everyone, including ourselves.

Fortunately, God knows who we *really* are. As with Gordon, our ability to know God and experience Him has much to do with our ability to know ourselves. Our "public" self cannot have a relationship with God, because God is truth and our "impostor" self is, in large part, a lie. In fact, it is that impostor that causes our doublemindedness, our instability, and all sorts of other problems that we create for ourselves.

The good news is, we can be ourselves with God. Since we are to meet God in an honest and genuine way, we don't have to hide or pretend or deceive Him (not that we could). Our motivation for an authentic relationship with God is love and not obligation or guilt or fear. That's why man-made religion doesn't help us, because it can too easily become *another* disguise, hiding who we really are in an effort to please people and play a social role. Thankfully, that's the last thing God wants. You can and should reveal every aspect of yourself to God—the good, the bad, and even the things you don't understand about yourself—because God already knows everything there is to know about you. And—it bears repeating—God loves you right here, right now, just the way you are! But who are you?

You Are Designed

You can't surprise God with who you are, because you were personally designed and planned by the Creator of all things long before you arrived on Planet Earth.

God intentionally designed your personality. He lovingly gave to you the special characteristics that are uniquely yours.

Do you wish you were taller? Shorter? Somehow different in coloring or body style or features? Do you wish you were an extrovert instead of an introvert, or vice versa? Do you have a disability and struggle to understand why you have to be "different"? Do you look like a lot of other people and wish you *were* a little different? Do you have a weird family, or an unusual ethnic mix, or a tendency to put on weight? Are you a has-been or a wannabe? In your efforts to fit the mold or to adapt to the world's ever-changing estimation of beauty or normalcy or success, you may have overlooked something very important: *you are designed exactly the way God wanted you to be.* Have you ever stopped to think about God's original design for you?

There is not another person just like you. There never has been and there never will be. Because God has placed within every created thing an interconnectedness, every person has a plan and a purpose. Think about that when you have doubts about your reason for existence: God thought you up and made you just the way you are for a reason. In fact, nothing has ever happened to you that hasn't happened for a reason.

Perhaps that idea causes you to say, "Wait a minute, do you know what I've been through? Don't tell me there was a reason! Don't try to convince me that tragedy is part of God's plan." We must remember that we are eternal, spiritual beings housed in a physical body. If you can change your perspective a little and see things through eternal and spiritual eyes, temporary, physical things tend to diminish. That doesn't minimize our pain. It doesn't mean it isn't difficult. It simply means that there are eternal and spiritual purposes to the things that happen to us that may, for the moment, extend beyond our capacity to understand.

There is not another person designed just like you. There is no other life planned and designed just like yours. There never has been and never will be. You fulfill a special and unique role in the universe—strength, weakness, beauty, imperfection, joy, heartache, and all.

You Are Created

You were a personal God-thought before you were ever born. You were created in God's imagination. God thought you up; He invented you. What do you like? Color? Music? People? Ideas? God made you that way, and if you'll watch carefully He will also bring things to your attention that He knows you will enjoy. His personal awareness of each of us, His attention to us, helps us see how important we are to Him; it provides us with personal worth and dignity.

Just as God created and knows the intimate details of your nature, He also has complete knowledge of His personal and perfect plan for you. In fact, only God knows exactly what it is. As we begin to focus our attention on knowing God and on allowing Him to help us know ourselves, we become more aware and alert to the twists and turns of our life's pathway. We begin to see, with eternal and spiritual eyes, the subtle lessons, meanings, and changes in direction that take place every day. As we come to know God and to know ourselves, we also come to know, at least in part, God's plans and purposes for our lives. And those plans and purposes are eternal.

For some of us, the idea of eternal life can be almost as scary as the alternative. "Eternity" can conjure up the fear of the unknown or worse, images of endless boredom. For some people who have experienced a great deal of heartache, eternity seems like an opportunity for a never-ending series of miserable experiences and disappointments.

It's helpful to think of eternity not as an endless amount of time, but as *timelessness*. Time is a device to measure experiences and nothing more. God operates outside of time. He just "IS." In fact, He calls Himself "I AM." Think about being "I AM" as opposed to "I WAS" or "I WILL BE."

Purposeful life belongs to those who live right now. If you believe that God can give eternal life to His human creation, you can immediately say that two of humankind's greatest enemies have been destroyed: *fear of the past and fear of the future.* Living in the present means living—right now—a purposeful, meaningful life.

However, since time and its limitations are still part of our lives, consider the fact that time is your friend and not your enemy. You are an eternal being, but God made you specifically for now, this place, this time. You can use time to heal your wounds. You can use it to distance yourself from past mistakes. Most of all, time provides you the opportunity to experience people, places, and things for one indispensable purpose, to *know* God.

Just as you were created as an eternal being in a physical body, you were also created with the ability to choose your thoughts. Much can be taken from us—our possessions, our comforts, our health, our freedom, our relationships. But no one can take from us what we choose to think. Sometimes choosing the right thoughts—positive instead of negative, "real you" instead of "imposter you"—is a discipline, and it can be a moment by moment process. If you let someone else choose for you what you will think about, then you are not honoring yourself or the love God has for you. *Think for yourself*, because your *thoughts* originate from one of God's most successful creative accomplishments—*your mind*.

You Are Loved

Just as it was God's nature as Creator that caused Him to make you, it is God's nature as Lover that causes Him to love you just the way He made you. God's unconditional love applies to every aspect of who you are right now. God won't love you more tomorrow after you've "cleaned up your act." God didn't love you more yesterday before things happened the way they did. *Because of who God is, He loves you unconditionally, not in spite of who you are, but because of who you are.* And God's unconditional love for you demonstrates how He also wants you to love yourself unconditionally. It bears repeating—*God is love.*

Because of the way God created me, I can see, sense, and feel God's love in everything and everyone He made: light, breath, nature, babies, laughter, energy, rain, sun, moon, butterflies, passion, sex. Maybe you can't see God's love in Charles Manson or Hitler, but you can see a lack of His love in them. When God's love isn't understood or received or given freely in the world, crime, tragedy, and devastation are the result.

All of God's love is available to you. Once you begin to enjoy the intimate side of this relationship, you begin to see the little personal gifts He gives you. God has given you the inner power to discover and explore what He wants you to know about Him. One of the most important things to know on your personal journey is that you don't have to go to someone else to find God. In fact, you really can't. God has given *you* the power and ability to discover Him for *yourself*. If we really want to know God and begin to seek Him wholeheartedly, it is an absolute certainty that we will find Him. Why? Because God has placed a part of Himself within everyone.

You Are a Receiver

You have received many gifts from God. You have received your personality, your mind, your physical body, and your best attributes. Some of the things you may not prize about yourself are gifts, too, once you see them for what they are. You have even received from God the freedom of choice to receive or reject His gifts to you. And the greatest gift God has given you is Himself. He created you in His image.

Being made in the image of God means different things to different people. Some people think of God's image as His attributes, characteristics that we share with God like creativity, love, wisdom, intelligence, or generosity. Others define the image of God as a "spark of divinity" that He lit in every human heart. Still others think that being made in the image of God means that God has engraved within every heart a natural law that compels us, by nature, to seek Him and to love one another.

Whenever we consider God's presence within us, we open our minds and hearts to new potential, new promise, new power, and new peace. In the next chapter we will look more closely at who we are when we acknowledge God's presence within us.

But sometimes there are barriers between us and God. There are attitudes and feelings and fears that block our way. Sometimes they have to do with our impostor-self. Sometimes they are defenses we have devised to protect ourselves from hurt. And sometimes they are simply misunderstandings about God's nature—baggage we don't need to carry with us on our quest.

OVERCOMING BARRIERS

During your MindFast, you will be given the opportunity to consider some of the things that you may be allowing to block your way to God. But for now, let me share with you something Tom Hicks has written about barriers. I think it is a great illustration of what every one of us deals with when we start facing who we really are. Tom describes a library containing books about our personal life.

Many unique and beautiful stories could be told about you and your experiences. Volumes of books could be written about you; in fact I can almost imagine that every one of us has an entire library of books written just about our unique story. There are books of LOVE, FAITH, COURAGE, and VICTORY in your library. However, there are also some books about FEAR, DOUBT, SHAME, HURT, and BITTER-NESS. Those books may cause you to cower, cry, be embarrassed, or feel depressed. All great books evoke emotion, which is a powerful human characteristic.

Try visualizing yourself in a big, comfortable room filled with books. For me, it is a light and airy room painted in California pastels with lots of sunlight and books stacked randomly around me. For Ron, it is a dark paneled affair with a huge leather chair and an Irish setter dozing in front of the fireplace. Whatever the ambiance, your library should be your special place.

Once you are totally relaxed, take the book entitled FEAR off the shelf and begin reading it to yourself. Make sure you don't skip over the scariest parts. My book titled FEAR starts with me falling down the stairs at five years old. It goes on to the first day of school. Getting caught on the gymnasium floor in my street shoes. Fighting a kid named Mike on the school playground. Bringing home a note to be signed by my parents from the teacher. My first date. The first time the police pulled me over in my car. Would I have to go to Vietnam? Having a "joint" handed to me in college. My first job interview. Getting married. Having kids. Starting my own business. Coping with business catastrophes. Fear of death. Fear of betrayal. Fear of disease. Fear of disaster. Is God there?

My heart is pounding, and my palms are sweaty. I need to take a breath. I think I'll put that book away. Let me see . . . hmm . . . I believe I'll read the VICTORY book now.

Five-year-old Tom falls down the stairs and lives. He is more careful next time. The first day of school Tom meets a new friend and loves his teacher. He looks forward to going to school the rest of the year. Tom gets punished for playing on gym floor in street shoes but gets asked to join basketball team. Tom fights Mike then becomes friends with him. Tom brings home the note from school and after Mom scolds him and signs it, she makes him his favorite dessert.

Tom's first date doesn't go well but his date's best friend becomes an ideal second date. The police scared Tom so badly that he still doesn't speed to this day. The Vietnam War ended, he didn't become addicted to marijuana, and he didn't get the first job he interviewed for, but he got another one. He dated a lot, broke some hearts, had his broken a time or two. Ultimately Tom married the most fantastic girl in the world. He had two beautiful children whom he adores. He has made and lost a lot of money and has lived to tell the tale.

Tom has lost friends and relatives along the way, but he has gained as many as he has lost. He has been betrayed by some of his closest associates and has been blessed by total strangers. For every physical ailment and natural disaster that he has experienced, there are at least a million that he has been spared. Throughout every circumstance of Tom's life, God is always there!

All in all, the VICTORY book is an amazing story of one miraculous character always landing on his feet, while the FEAR book is about a pitiful, paralyzed waif. I feel sympathy for him. You may have noticed that in the VICTORY book, fear was allowed to participate. In fact, fear was a player and was used to assist VICTORY. However, in the FEAR book, victory had no place. Fear reigned supreme.

God has filled your library with many books. You will like the stories. They will reveal to you a lot of inside information about someone that you should get to know intimately—you! When you are finished reading one of your books, dis-

cuss it with God. With Him, you can laugh, cry, shout with joy, or simply reflect on the ironies. The rich, complicated depth of this person called you can only be fully understood when God explains the chaos that sometimes appears on the surface and may even seem to block the way. It will take many visits to your personal library to discover the answers, but it is a place where you and God can meet together. And that's exactly where you want to be.

Chapter Four

WHO ARE YOU AND GOD TOGETHER?

Infinite riches in a little room.
—MARLOWE

The time is nearly here for your journey toward Ground Zero to begin, but there's one more question I'd like to raise before you start your MindFast. We've reflected upon who God is. We've taken some time to think about who you are. *But who are you and God together?*

This is a question that will require more from you than any other, because only you can discover that specific answer. We can share with you some ideas and some discoveries of our own. But there is no other combination on earth quite like you matched up with God. Just stop and think again about yourself as a unique and wonderful creation. Isn't it incredible that you were created to be the one-of-a-kind, irreplaceable person you are? Now add to the equation God's awesome presence in your life. The very best thing you can imagine in all the world is the combination of those two things—you and God together.

Exciting as the possibilities are, that idea may cause you to cringe. One of the things we've learned from our Ground Zero interviews was that almost everyone said, "Oh, no! God couldn't love me!" A terrible sense of unworthiness floods our minds when we think about the God of the universe living inside us. We know ourselves far too well. We are quite aware of who we are and what we do in secret. And we fully recognize that God knows too. Does it surprise you to hear that God loves you anyway? Believe it or not, God wants to be a part of your life more than anything in the world.

You need God, whether you want to admit it or not. Every one of us has a God-shaped hole in our life, and we try to fill it up with everything imaginable: money, sex, success, drugs and alcohol, family, beauty, health. But that "God-shaped vacuum" will always be empty and aching, because nothing can fill it except God. We have an eternal spirit that longs to reconnect with our Maker, and it won't be satisfied with substitutes. We will always be yearning for God until we realize that God also has a jealous craving for us that is only filled when we are one with Him.

Even if you're feeling unworthy or afraid or doubtful, keep reading. You'll have a chance to take a look at those blockages and barriers a little later. For now, be assured that there is *nothing* in your heart that God can't deal with. There is *nothing* that can surprise Him or shock Him. There is *nothing* in your mind, in your imagination, in your past, or anywhere else in the universe powerful enough to keep Him from loving you and wanting to share Himself with you.

WE ARE DESIGNED DESIGNERS

Sometimes when we talk about one person being in love with another, we say, "He (or she) has designs on you." That's a very good expression to use to describe God's love, because God has designs on you; He designed you and created you to share His image in the world. And as you recognize God in your life, you start to see things differently; the world around you seems to have a different design from before.

You begin to see with spiritual eyes. You begin to think God's thoughts. You learn to develop an eternal perspective and to add a spiritual dimension to your point of view. Naturally, this kind of personal transformation is a process, it's not something that happens overnight. But change *will* come, and you'll never be the same. You will become the designer, like your Creator, of good acts, good thoughts, good words, good gifts, and good relationships. God is good!

God-in-you means that you are actually able to think God-thoughts—thoughts that provide inspiration, imagination, motivation, and dreams. Sometimes it means you have a brilliant new idea. Sometimes it means you wake up in the night, concerned about someone you love and are reminded to pray. Sometimes it means that you are moved, beyond explanation, to go somewhere, to provide something, to give a gift, or to offer help. You may even find yourself doing the very last thing you ever planned to do.

You've probably heard it said, "You may be the only picture of God someone sees today." That's more true than you can imagine, because when God is working through you, you actually become God's hands and feet and eyes and ears and mouth. God uses all sorts of different people to bless, to speak, to listen. By working through people like you and me, God's thoughts are carried out here on earth. When I have the inspiration to do something, I need to pay attention to my impulse. It may well be God's nudge, sending me out to do His creative business.

WE ARE CREATED CREATORS

Maybe the word *creative* sounds a little strange to you. You might be the first to admit that you don't see yourself as a creative person. But creativity isn't just about art projects and music and writing plays or poems. There is creativity in the way your personality plays out. The way you speak, the way you smile, the way you touch others are all part of your created purpose.

God created you so that you and He could do things together. No matter how little "talent" you may think you have, God's creativity works through you anyway. Whenever you do something well and you know you're doing just what you're supposed to be doing, it makes you feel happy, fulfilled, and glad to be alive. That is the "Big Guy" letting you know that you're doing just what you were created to do. When you accomplish the things you were designed and created to do, peace and joy will spill out of you.

Even if you don't think you are creative, you may be surprised to see what happens when God brings out the best in you. God-in-you can give you the ability to create something from your thoughts, just as God created you from His thoughts. You may find yourself with an all new interest in music, art, woodworking, theater, designing, gardening, or writing. You may discover hidden talents that you never recognized before. The combination of you and God is totally unique. There is no other unique being exactly like "God-in-you"—never has been, never will be. You are a demonstration of His design, His creative genius, and His love.

We Are Loved Lovers

God has put His love in all creation and in all people. God's love in us allows us to see and experience His love in others. God expects you to pass on to others the unconditional love you and He share together. The more you're aware of His love in you, the more natural it is for you to see it in others. It's impossible to give unconditional love without knowing God, because the only time we can really love unconditionally is when it is God doing it through us. In our human state, I don't think we can love without strings attached; even when God loves through us, it's difficult. Yet the universal law of love couldn't be more clear: love God, love yourself, love each other.

It's only when you and I know how much God loves us, only when we know what unique creations we are in Him, that we are able to become secure enough to love someone else without worrying whether they are going to reciprocate and love us back. The more of God's love we allow to grow and flourish inside us, the more we have to give to those who need to receive His love.

WE ARE GIVEN GIVERS

God gives generously to us again and again and again, and we don't always see His gifts for what they are. But it is important for us to realize how much we have been given, because only then are we able to share it with others.

We have been given life, breath, talents, health, looks, friends, intelligence, family, food, shelter, ideas, dreams, and countless blessings, both great and small. There is nothing in our lives, in fact, that we have not been given. God gives to us constantly, in unique and unexpected ways. He gives us loving tokens of Himself that only we can understand.

Dee Kimbrell tells a wonderful story of a special gift God gave to her during a very difficult time:

> One of my very best friends was thirty-five years old when she learned that she had ovarian cancer. For the first time in my life, someone I loved, someone I knew intimately was going to die "before her time." I fought and argued with God, telling Him again and again that she was not supposed to die. When I finally accepted that it was going to happen anyway, I raged and screamed at Him. I begged Him to show me that He was really there.
>
> Then, at what appeared to be the worst possible

time, I was scheduled to go on a beach trip with my family. I didn't want to leave home because my friend was so very sick, and I was afraid she would die while I was gone. What happened next was completely unexpected—a treasured gift that could only have come from God to me.

I had grown up in Florida. Every time I went to the beach there as a child, I looked for sand dollars. I never found one, but I always looked for them anyway. It had even crossed my mind before we left on this trip that it would be really wonderful if I found a sand dollar.

On the second day of our beach holiday, my son and I saw some people gathered on a sand bar. Curious, we went out to see what they were doing. When we got there, I found not one or two, but thirty-three sand dollars! I could hardly believe my eyes. And in my heart, I kept hearing the same words over and over, "I have so many good gifts for you. I have so many good gifts for you."

As Dee discovered, God gives generously to every person, and He wants us to be givers, too, to pass the blessings along. But we need to keep our eyes open, to be alert and aware so that we don't miss the precious, personal gifts He offers us. It may be more than a gift. It may be a message. It may be the opportunity of a lifetime. Or it may just be God saying, "Hi." But when we begin to see God in everything, from that moment on, God is no longer a concept, God is someone we *know* by experience.

One of the things God has given us are promises. When God promises something, He can be trusted to keep His word. And God has promised that He will never leave us or forsake us. That means that His presence will not only remain within us, but that we can be sure that we are surrounded by God's presence at all times, in all places.

Feeling God's presence is wonderful, but feelings can come and go, and the *fact* of His presence is constant. God's presence is reality, and as we grow and search for Him, we become grounded in that fact rather than relying on our feelings. If you get distracted or wander off in the wrong direction, you may stop "feeling" God's presence. But no matter how far away you may feel from God, you can be sure of this: *He has not moved. Only you have.*

In the next section of the book, you will find the map for your MindFast. It will help you discover, without interference from anyone else, who God is, who you are, and who you and God are together. You will have the opportunity to reflect, to write your thoughts, and to explore questions you may not have thought about before. I think, by the time you've completed the process, you will have discovered answers to some of your deepest questions.

Before you begin, I thought you might enjoy hearing from someone who has walked the road before you. Wanda Denny describes her own experience at a Ground Zero MindFast retreat. With wisdom and good humor, she has generously shared with us glimpses of her own quest for God and what she discovered along the way. By the time you've finished reading her reflections, I'm pretty sure you're going to be ready to begin your own journey toward Ground Zero.

STARTING AT GROUND ZERO

WHAT IS GROUND ZERO? *My friend who told me about the retreat knew little about the concept. "They're hanging out with God in nature," she said. "But I don't think it's religious," another friend added. But God in nature? That made me a little nervous. "Wait," I said. "Is this one of those quests where you spend three days in the wilderness without food and you start to see things? Where rocks have smiling faces and talk to you? That kind of wilderness weekend?" I asked. My friend wasn't sure.*

But she knew it was a weekend retreat at picturesque Center Hill Lake in middle Tennessee—a place I knew well from childhood, from those end-of-summer, school's-about-to-start camping trips. The October weather was crisp. I had no definite plans for the weekend. And I was moving into a new home in two weeks and in dire need of a pre-stress-buster weekend, like taking two preventive aspirin before going out New Year's Eve.

So I read Ron Cook's bio. The brochure listed him as the retreat "leader." He's president of Legends Management Group, a company he founded with Danny White, former Dallas Cowboys quarterback. Legends represents retired NFL quarterbacks and connects them to entertainment and corporate projects. From his picture I could tell Ron was a boomer (baby boomer, that is). Grasping at straws to find a connection, I took comfort in knowing I had something in common with Ron, even if it was age related.

In spite of my hesitation, I felt a strong urge to go on the retreat. Maybe it was because of the retreat's name. Ground Zero: a crystallization of my life. I'm in transition after being downsized from a managerial job. Though I miss the salary, I don't miss corporate America. I'll start film school in January, preparing for a new career as a film producer/director/writer. My old life is over. My new life is sprouting from new seed. It's really an exciting time in my life. But my old life ended before my new life started, which is not the way I would have planned. Did God make a mistake there? Anyway, there I was: Ground Zero. I decided to sign up.

Armed with sketchy information and major curiosity, I drove sixty-five miles from Nashville to Smithville on a gorgeous Saturday morning. As I drove, I reasoned that if this retreat didn't work out, I would drive to a nearby town, spend the weekend with my friends Bobby and Kim, and shop for five-dollar shoes at a discount store. The weekend retreat might be cool, but if they tried to "save me," I was outta there.

When I arrived at Lakeside Resort, I was met by three warm, smiling faces, huddled around a card table under a shade tree. Their welcome was genuine and cordial. Ron Cook, Dee Kimbrell, and Tom Hicks immediately alleviated my fears with their enthusiasm and assurance of a fun-filled, spiritually rich weekend.

After settling in to the rustic cabin, I skipped off to the amphitheater for the first meeting. With map in hand, I could see the amphitheater but had no clue how to get there, which is a metaphor for life, eh? It looked like I'd get there if I went straight down an embankment, over a gully, and straight down a steep grade. On with the quest.

Bravely, I made my way to the amphitheater, sliding and slipping in new leather-bottom sandals. The outdoor theater with neatly manicured green grass and wooden benches was filling up with attendees. I had my choice of shade or beaming brilliant sunshine. I opted for shade, fearing more wrinkles and overexposure. I'd left the house without my Estee Lauder.

The fall weather complemented the retreat. The lake was sky blue and was dotted with water-skiers and boat enthusiasts.

The time had come for us to find out what Ground Zero was all about. Ron Cook said that the Ground Zero format is unstructured. The program focus, he said, is on developing a close relationship with God, a notion that terrifies most people. I looked around; no one here seemed terrified. Our first assignment was to spend some time alone in nature while pondering three questions: Who is God? Who are you? Who are the two of you together? "Don't worry about coming back with answers," Ron said. "Just think about those questions for a while." We dismissed and, sandals in hand, I headed for the water's edge.

I plopped down on my yoga mat with my favorite twenty-nine-cent purple ink pen and purple doodling pad to think about those questions. I sat and sat. And sat and sat. I was bored. I had been sitting on my mat for ten minutes. Fatigue wouldn't come. My mind was kicking *and screaming for something to occupy the time.* Great, *I thought.* A weekend doing nothing. What a waste of my time. *I was moving in two weeks and hadn't packed the first book. I had agreed to attend this retreat where it looked like we were going to do nothing for an entire weekend! What had I done?*

I was beginning to outline a new business strategy when a clump of wild daisies caught my eye. I began to feel a little guilty about working. Ron had asked us to leave the "stuff" at home for the next twenty-four hours. Couldn't I do that?

Restless, I tried to nap, hike, and people watch. I practiced writing with my left hand to trigger my intuition. Twenty minutes passed. Okay, God. *My ego was screaming for attention. Then, from out of nowhere, serenity infused my veins. Tranquillity. Peace.* Hello, God. I want to know You, God, so start talking.

No answer came, no voice. What am I supposed to do? *You're doing it! Film school in January.* What am I to do in the meantime? Did You forget about the money for my tuition? What about my car insurance? Where is that money coming from? *A voice from within said:* You are fine. Be here with the retreat. Be here.

I must have dozed off. An hour had passed, and it was time to return to the amphitheater for the next set of contemplative questions.

Session two focused on "Who am I?" An interesting question, but why do I need to know that? Back to the woods. The session was shortened to about a half-hour. Yea! I'd gotten a reprieve.

I sat on the boat dock ramp anticipating the sunset. I

was fleetingly aware of my deeply relaxed state. That sunset was majestic, just like when I was a kid. The sunset hues probably hadn't changed in a million years. That sunset of God's. Made for me. The sunset and I, both created by God. God the artist. God the parent, always looking out for me, always within me.

I was moving to a new home, going to film school, but those changes are external. The God within me is constant. There on the boat dock I had a holy moment of knowing I was safe and secure regardless of my unknown future.

Later we feasted on a campfire dinner of burgers, chicken, and grilled cookies (a guy thing—they grill any and everything). I've eaten chicken a thousand times in my life but in this heightened state of awareness, I tasted chicken for the first time. We ate on linen tablecloths covering a stone picnic table. I flashed back to a memory of roadside parks before the days of interstate highways.

My heart was gay. I felt unhurried and not a bit anxious. Maybe there was something to this solitude, this sit in the woods stuff. Being with God in nature.

Through a powerful telescope, I studied Saturn with the rings. How many rings does Saturn have? There were no clouds in the dark vast sky. Stars were popping into view seemingly out of nowhere. How many other galaxies were out there? The expansive nature of the universe intrigued me. That big universe out there and little old me. Yet I felt completely whole. Boundless nature. Unlimited possibilities.

The next morning I walked to the boat dock in the

pink glow of dawn. Wow! Childhood memories flooded me when I saw the campfire roaring beside the water's edge. I suddenly, painfully missed my daddy who has been gone for five years. We are bonded together always. He'll meet me when I pass on and will show me the ropes. I feel at peace with dying. God is there for me now and for always. I grooved on this thought while I watched Planet Earth come to life.

A crackling campfire. Coffee. Cool breezes blowing from the lake. Peace. I fit. There is a plan for me. Don't know what it will hold, exactly. But that doesn't matter. God put me here to go to film school, to be here beside this lake, to hold this cup of coffee in my hands and feel the wind blow through my hair. Does God care if I ever win an Academy Award? God knows my heart's desire. And God gave me this mind, this amazing mind.

Then it was time for breakfast. I was hungry for some eggs.

Laughing, joking, bonding with the group. We were joined together by our wilderness experience! I care about those people. I wanted to know them better, to touch them, to see them again. I want the very best for them, as God wants the best for me. Insight: I am not forgotten by God.

The last session began and I felt sad, a loss that "camp" was over, that I had to go back home. A worry about a bank deposit hit me like a lightning bolt. Stay cool, I remind myself. God is bigger than my bank deposit. God is my supply.

Back to the woods to contemplate me and God. What is our partnership? Danged if I know. I know I'm not cool enough to hang with God. I don't deserve to partner with God. "Yes, you do, My beloved child." Oh, great. Now I was hearing voices. Like I'm not stressed enough. Now I have to stagger through the streets of Nashville hallucinating that God and I are partners. Will I be locked up?

In an instant that's indescribable, something in my chest region went Pop. A letting go. A release. Tears were spurting, pouring. Clean, pure tears of joy. Suddenly I was lighter.

During the wrap session somehow I was more present. Words were not as important. There were hints from the group about feeling lighter for the experience. I was eager to continue on this path of doing . . . what was this? Doing nothing. Doing nothing with God. I resolved to walk the Ground Zero twenty-eight-day road to greater intimacy with God. Count on me to spread the word. I'm willing to pitch my baggage, erroneous thinking, and start from Ground Zero in building a new relationship with my Father.

But one last thing, God. About my school tuition . . . (Sorry, old habits die hard!)

Journal of Days

Week One: Who Is God?

Week Two: Who Are You?

Week Three: What's Blocking the Way?

Week Four: Who Are You and God Together?

Ground Zero

Journal of Days

MONDAY

WEEK ONE: WHO IS GOD?

DAY TWENTY-EIGHT

We know that God is Spirit. He is Love and Light and Life. Nonetheless, some of us have mental images of God in our minds, and some of these inaccurate ideas can affect our efforts to seek and really know God.

Some people picture God as an old, old man or a Santa Claus–type of character. Others envision the historical Jesus, dressed in ancient Israeli robes and sandals. Still others imagine a hardhearted king, decked out in priceless jewels and riding in a chariot.

On day twenty-eight of our MindFast, we are going to reflect upon the mental image of God that we keep somewhere in our minds and imaginations. Who or what do we have in mind when we think about God?

Relax.
Listen.
God is with you right here, right now.

Today and every day that follows, please write your thoughts and responses to the following questions. Later on you will be asked to review your answers.

MORNING
How do you picture God in your mind?

MIDDAY
Where does God live? How do you picture this place in your mind?

EVENING
What does the voice of God sound like to you?

Journal of Days

TUESDAY

WEEK ONE: WHO IS GOD?

DAY TWENTY-SEVEN

Whatever your ideas about God may be today, chances are they were influenced by something or someone in your past. During your MindFast, it's important for you to set aside your preconceived ideas and begin to seek God and think about Him on your own.

Parents and family have much to do with your early impressions of God. You will, for example, struggle with accepting the idea of "Father God" if your own father was unkind, uncaring, or even abusive. Likewise, you may have difficulties with a God who loves uncondi- tionally if you have been inconsistently loved in your family.

If your parents and family are devoutly religious, you will have been brought up with their ideas, some of which may be very good and helpful. Others may not. If you have no religious background, you may have absorbed some vague concepts of God, perhaps without even realizing it, from film or fiction or philosophy.

But do your ideas about God reflect the real God? Your MindFast will prepare you to meet God personally and to discover who God really is.

Relax.
Listen.
God is with you right here, right now.

Write your thoughts and responses to the following questions.

MORNING
Who taught you most of what you believe about God? When? How?

MIDDAY
Which aspects of what you believe about God were *personal* discoveries? Describe those discoveries.

EVENING
When you think about God, do you feel that God is a friend, an acquaintance, or a stranger? Explain.

Journal of Days

WEDNESDAY

WEEK ONE: WHO IS GOD?

DAY TWENTY-SIX

Believing in God and believing in a personal, loving God are two different things.

Just as some of us have a mental idea of God as an exceptionally powerful human being, others may think of God as an impersonal, cosmic force, a positively charged energy field, or a Creator who set the universe in motion and then lost interest in the creation.

During your MindFast, it is important for you to take time away from other people, phones, faxes, TVs, and other noisy distractions. Once alone and quiet, you can take a look inside yourself and see what comes to mind when you think about drawing close to God and getting to know Him better.

Relax.
Listen.
God is with you right here, right now.

Write your thoughts and responses to the following questions.

MORNING

Have you ever been totally alone with God? Why or why not? What good things might happen if you were alone with God? What might be the challenges?

MIDDAY

Write three personal questions you would want to ask God in a face-to-face meeting. There are no rules. You can ask the "Big Guy" anything you want.

EVENING

What is keeping you from having an intimate and personal relationship with God? What do you think you could do about it?

Journal of Days

THURSDAY

WEEK ONE: WHO IS GOD?

DAY TWENTY-FIVE

Our interest in knowing God is rarely intellectual or academic. Most of us cherish an intense personal desire to experience God's presence in our lives. We hope to gain from God understanding about our existence and our purpose in life. We long for God's help with the problems and challenges we face. We desire a connection with the Master Artist who made all the beauties of nature, who set the universe in motion, who designed every mountain ridge and river and rainbow. Sometimes we want to thank God for the good things we've received; sometimes we want to talk to God about our losses.

As you take the time to seek God on our own, you may find that you already have some very specific ideas about who God is and what He does. Many people believe, for example, that God causes amazing and unexplainable things to happen; most people pray when they need help. And nearly everyone assumes God is *somewhere*—near or far, alive in our hearts or watching us from a distance.

Relax.
Listen.
God is with you right here, right now.

Write your thoughts and responses to the following questions.

MORNING
Do you feel that God is *inside* you or *outside* and separate from you? Is God close and all around or distant and far away?

MIDDAY
Remember a time when you asked God for something and describe the answer you received.

EVENING
Describe an "unexplainable" coincidence that recently happened in your life.

Journal of Days

FRIDAY

WEEK ONE: WHO IS GOD?

DAY TWENTY-FOUR

A s the Master Creator of all things, God's finger-prints can be found on every part of nature. As the One who holds all things together, God's power is evident in everything that surrounds us. Even though we may struggle to picture God in our minds—it is hard to envision a spirit—we are able to discover God in His handiwork, which reflects His nature.

Many of God's attributes are present in nature: power, beauty, and creativity. Scripture actually describes God as *love* and *light* and *life*. Although we cannot fully grasp the fullness of God's personality with our human minds, we can catch glimpses of Him from the things He has made and from the things He has done for us.

Relax.
Listen.
God is with you right here, right now.

Write your thoughts and responses to the following questions.

MORNING
What aspects of nature do you love most? Why?

MIDDAY
Have you ever felt God's presence in a force of nature? Explain. What in nature most vividly reveals God to you?

EVENING
In our interviews we found that many people had a "fan club" relationship with God. They are familiar with all the songs, they've been to several concerts, they know lots of facts about Him, but they can't say that they really know Him personally. What's the difference between really knowing God and just knowing about God?

Journal of Days

WEEKEND

WEEK ONE: WHO IS GOD?

DAYS TWENTY-THREE AND TWENTY-TWO

Learning to be alone is an important element in our search for God. Some people crave isolation, but others can't bear to be by themselves. No doubt we have good reasons for our various responses to solitude.

If we are not at peace with ourselves, we may not be comfortable in the company of our own thoughts. Solitude alarms us. On the other hand, some of us habitually avoid being in contact with other people and are forever in search of isolation and privacy. Sometimes this is simply the result of shyness, but too often it takes place because of deep discomfort with other people—people who could annoy, anger, hurt, disappoint, or reopen our unhealed wounds.

Whatever your view of solitude, you must have silence and time alone in order to draw near to God. That's why your MindFast requires you to withdraw yourself, temporarily, from all but God. Later, when you return to the company of others, you will be able to know them better and love them more, because the One who made you is able to teach you to love yourself as well as everybody else.

Relax.
Listen.
God is with you right here, right now.

BOTH MORNINGS

Spend some time in complete solitude. Review your notes from the past week, and ask God to share His thoughts with you about what He may have been saying. Relax. Be still. Listen.

BOTH AFTERNOONS

Deliberately choose activities that are relaxing and as stress-free as possible. If possible, turn off the cell phone and the beeper. Breathe deeply. Concentrate on slowing down your pace and your mind. Give thanks for everything beautiful you see around you.

FIELD TRIP

As soon as possible, go to a local hospital and spend thirty minutes looking at the new babies, parents, nurses, and friends of the families. Just observe. Where does new life originate? What does the birth of a child tell you about God? Reflect on experiences in your life that brought new life to you.

Journal of Days

MONDAY

WEEK TWO: WHO ARE YOU?

DAY TWENTY-ONE

Each of us is a special individual, formed in the mind of God, designed before the world began. We are all different. No two people can think exactly the same thoughts, develop totally identical ideas, or accomplish the same things. The reason for our uniqueness is the immense creativity of God: God's mind is forever creating new life, and every one of us is a unique "God-thought."

As you take time to reflect upon yourself as God's intentional design, you will be able to see a purpose in the various attributes and qualities that make up who you are. Today you will begin to reflect on who you are, why you are the way you are, and what being a "God-thought" really means.

Relax.
Listen.
God is with you right here, right now.

Write your thoughts and responses to the following questions.

MORNING
Try to imagine that you were once a thought of God's. Describe what that means to you.

MIDDAY
Think about it: you had nothing to do with any of the circumstances of your birth—your parents, the time, the place, your sex, your face, your physical body. Write your thoughts about this.

EVENING
Since God "thought you up" and made you exactly the way you are for a reason, don't you think God wants to share His thoughts about you—His personal creation? Listen carefully, then write what you think God might be saying to you.

Journal of Days

TUESDAY

WEEK TWO: WHO ARE YOU?

DAY TWENTY

Once we realize that God is love and light and life, we begin to understand that His creation of each of us was an act of goodness and delight. God was happier on the day you were born than you can imagine. God was pleased just as you are pleased when you finish a project that requires your creativity.

Sometimes we don't look on ourselves with pleasure. Our thoughts about ourselves may focus on what we consider to be flaws or imperfections that keep us from feeling grateful to God for thinking of us and creating us. We may even allow our negative thoughts about ourselves to blind us to the fact that we are a "God-thought."

By concentrating our attention on God's love, you can begin to see His creation of you in a different light. You can start to realize that you were made for God's pleasure. God brought you into the world to bless His creation with your unique existence.

Relax.
Listen.
God is with you right here, right now.

Write your thoughts and responses to the following questions.

MORNING
List three things about yourself that you are thankful for. List three other things about yourself that you need to learn to value more or to develop more fully.

MIDDAY
Because you are unlike anyone else, your thoughts are uniquely yours. Do you think your thoughts are special to God? Why or why not?

EVENING
What are the factors that you believe control your thoughts? List some of them. How much control do you have over your thoughts?

Journal of Days

WEDNESDAY

WEEK TWO: WHO ARE YOU?

DAY NINETEEN

J ust as the uniqueness of every human being tells us something about God's immense creativity, the circumstances of our birth tell us something about God's intentions. Wouldn't the God who designed the complexities of chemistry, mathematics, light, and sound have a plan for the crown of His creation—individual human beings?

The very fact that you were created in the "image of God" speaks of some reason for your existence that goes far beyond chance or random accident. Why would the Creator instill in every created individual a resemblance to Himself? Today you will begin to reflect on what God had in mind when He made you.

Relax.
Listen.
God is with you right here, right now.

Write your thoughts and responses to the following questions.

MORNING
Think about it: since the beginning of time, there has *never* been anyone exactly like you. Others may have similar traits, but no other person has ever had all the combined characteristics that make one very unique creation—you. Why do you think God chose to make you just the way you are?

MIDDAY
You had no choice in the circumstances of your birth, but God did. Describe your thoughts and feelings when you consider that you have been created with a plan and for a purpose.

EVENING
What does the phrase "created in God's image" mean to you? What part of His image could be a part of you?

Journal of Days

THURSDAY

WEEK TWO: WHO ARE YOU?

DAY EIGHTEEN

The idea that God wants to communicate with His creation is difficult for some people to believe. But look at it this way: if you can believe that God "thought you up" and made you exactly as you are for a reason, don't you think God also wants to share His thoughts with you?

If a unique path has been provided for your journey, don't you need a guide? If you are created for a purpose, with a plan in mind, surely God wants to help you find your way and to encourage you as you go.

Hearing from God is an important part of your MindFast; it is, in fact, the main reason you are setting time aside to listen. Today, I hope you'll open your ears, your heart, and your mind to whatever He may be saying.

Relax.
Listen.
God is with you right here, right now.

Write your thoughts and responses to the following questions.

MORNING
Think about what it would be like for the Creator and Designer of the universe to share His thoughts with you personally. You are a God-thought.

MIDDAY
Do you really believe that God shares His thoughts with us? How do you think He might do this?

EVENING
Where do your thoughts come from? How would you know if God were speaking to you in your mind?

Journal of Days

FRIDAY

WEEK TWO: WHO ARE YOU?

DAY SEVENTEEN

As quickly as the days fly by, the seasons change, and the children grow, we begin to realize that life is really much too short. When we contemplate how quickly time passes, we begin to wonder what happens after this life is over. Peggy Lee once sang, "Is that all there is?" We ask ourselves, "Or is there more?" Thankfully, there is *much* more. In fact, this brief life on earth is only the beginning.

Once you begin to see yourself as an *eternal* being, your view of yourself will change, and you will gain a new understanding of God's reasons for having created you. Adjusting your perspectives about time and eternity provides you with a God's-eye view of your life, your purpose, and the loving plan that existed for you long before the world was ever made.

Relax.
Listen.
God is with you right here, right now.

Write your thoughts and responses to the following questions.

MORNING
How would you define *eternity?* What do you personally believe happens after physical death?

MIDDAY
Do you believe that you are an eternal being in a physical body? How does being an eternal being change your view of yourself?

EVENING
Think back over your life as far as you can: What is your first memory? Why do you think that is the first thing that you can remember? What is your earliest memory of a connection with God?

Journal of Days

WEEKEND

WEEK TWO: WHO ARE YOU?

DAYS SIXTEEN AND FIFTEEN

Perhaps after two weeks of reflection and contemplation, the questions "Who is God?" and "Who are you?" now bring to mind some entirely new thoughts and ideas, things you've never thought about before. You may have gained a deeper appreciation of nature, or of beauty, or of God as love and light and life and Spirit. Or you may have simply come to see that, because of God's goodness, your life and your presence in the world have a far deeper and more satisfying meaning.

Today and tomorrow, I hope you'll take a few minutes to review some of the things you've thought and written and that you'll make sure you have some quiet time set aside for listening.

Most of all, I hope you'll set time aside for solitude and silence. These two key elements will help you more than anything else in completing the first part of your quest and, at the end, reaching the new beginning that we call Ground Zero.

Relax.
Listen.
God is with you right here, right now.

BOTH MORNINGS

Spend time in complete solitude. Review your notes from the past week, and ask God to share His thoughts with you about what He may have been saying. Relax. Be still. Listen.

BOTH AFTERNOONS

Deliberately choose a quiet, stress-free environment. Just as you did last weekend, once again turn off the cell phone and the beeper. Take deep breaths and consciously slow down. Give thanks that God made you—just the way you are.

FIELD TRIP

Find a wooded area or an isolated hill away from noise and "people activities." Be still and watch God at work. Try not to overlook even the smallest creatures under your feet or the wild birds soaring over your head. What does all the activity tell you about God? Think about how God watches over all His creation and how He is watching over you right now. Listen with your heart and see what He might be saying.

Journal of Days

MONDAY

WEEK THREE: WHAT'S BLOCKING THE WAY?

DAY FOURTEEN

Worry is a huge waste of time and energy, and it is the most counterproductive mental activity on earth. So why do we worry? Most of us don't trust anyone but ourselves with our anxieties and concerns. Others worry simply because it is a bad habit that hasn't been broken yet.

Fear is much like worry, but it is usually more intense and more focused. We may fear death, disease, financial disaster, disappointment, or some other "possibility." As with worries, our fears are usually far more damaging to us than the threats that create them. Our fears begin to own us, and we are unable to enjoy life because of them.

As we seek God and try to listen for God's words and wisdom, fearful and worried thoughts can intrude on us, distracting us from our focus and diverting our attention to an endless list of "what if's." The best way to keep our minds on God is to give our anxieties and fears to Him. A God who is wise, great, and loving can handle anything that comes and even turn it to our advantage. So, as the saying goes, "Give your worries to God before you go to bed. He's going to be up all night anyway."

Relax.
Listen.
God is with you right here, right now.

Write your thoughts and responses to the following questions.

MORNING
When you are trying to focus your mind on God, thoughts of all kinds may come in and interrupt your thinking. What are most of these thoughts about?

MIDDAY
Worries and fears are not unusual, but it can be an enormous drain on you mentally, emotionally, and spiritually. List the worries and fears that most frequently occupy your mind.

EVENING
One woman told me that every day she gives God her "anxious" thoughts in balloons. She described her mental process of placing her worries and fears in imaginary balloons and watching them float out of her sight into God's hands. Do the same; put each of your fears and worries in balloons and release them to God.

Journal of Days

TUESDAY

WEEK THREE: WHAT'S BLOCKING THE WAY?

DAY THIRTEEN

The expression "beyond the shadow of a doubt" is an apt description because doubts cast shadows across everything on our path. Doubt blocks the light and love of God and keeps us from listening and hearing from Him. In fact, if we allow it to, doubt can even block the way to our destination.

Some of our doubts are the result of things people have said to us, while others reflect difficult questions that remain unanswered or disappointments that have wounded us deeply. Facing doubts and calling them by name can eventually help us remove them from our thoughts. In order to hear God's thoughts, we have to silence the noisy voices of doubt that keep us from listening.

Relax.
Listen.
God is with you right here, right now.

Write your thoughts and responses to the following questions.

MORNING

As you try to think about God, you may have some serious questions about God's existence, about God's personal concern for you, or about God's goodness. What are your most serious doubts about God?

MIDDAY

Has something caused you to doubt God? Was it a disappointment? An intellectual argument? The words of someone else? Describe the source of your doubt and how it affects your quest to know God.

EVENING

Ask God to give you some thoughts that will help you overcome your doubts. Sit quietly for a few minutes, then write down whatever comes to mind.

Journal of Days

WEDNESDAY

WEEK THREE: WHAT'S BLOCKING THE WAY?

DAY TWELVE

Shame can be a huge obstacle in the lives of people who want to know God. Shame causes us to feel unworthy, unlovable, and too unrighteous to deal either with God or with people who seem "better" than we are.

Sometimes shame is placed on us by others. Sometimes it happens because we are subjected to a shameful environment. And sometimes it results from an isolated incident, which has caused us to feel disgraced. Since shame makes us feel unacceptable, most of us who live with feelings of shame have a very hard time reaching out to God or listening to what God might say to us. We imagine—wrongly—that God will either reject us or accuse us. In no way can we imagine God loving us unconditionally, just the way we are.

As you reach out to God, God will help you to identify the source of your feelings of shame. God wants you to be free from the emotional bondage caused by shame, and He will help you find that freedom—if you'll let Him.

Relax.
Listen.
God is with you right here, right now.

Write your thoughts and responses to the following questions.

MORNING
What specific situation in your life causes (or has caused) you to feel shame? Why?

MIDDAY
What does shame feel like to you? Describe your shameful feelings and write about a conversation, pardon, or some other intervention that you think might relieve them.

EVENING
If you could sit down with God and tell Him about your shame, what do you think He would say to you? Write down your thoughts about this.

Journal of Days

THURSDAY

WEEK THREE: WHAT'S BLOCKING THE WAY?

DAY ELEVEN

Hurt comes to us in many forms. It often is the result of loss. It may happen because of betrayal or misunderstanding or careless words. Or our hurt may be part of an ongoing situation that never seems to change. Whatever the source of your pain, it can get in the way of your quest to know God. For whatever reason, you are unable to get beyond it. You might say that although you are in deep need of healing, you can't quite find your way to the Healer.

Today we will take a few moments to reflect upon the pain we sometimes feel, to consider our response to it, and to see how it can block our way to Ground Zero. Pain rarely goes away all at once, but if we are able to see beyond it, we can gain hope. That hope will strengthen us and empower us to continue moving forward.

Relax.
Listen.
God is with you right here, right now.

Write your thoughts and responses to the following questions.

MORNING

Describe the most recent, painful hurt you have experienced (there may have been more than one). Are you still feeling that pain today? Explain.

MIDDAY

Sometimes when we are hurting, we become angry at God for letting something bad happen to us. Write a note to God about your hurt and tell Him how you feel. You can say anything to God you want to.

EVENING

How could anything good come out of your hurt? Hard as it is, try to imagine at least one positive result coming from your hurt. Describe it.

Journal of Days

FRIDAY

WEEK THREE: WHAT'S BLOCKING THE WAY?

DAY TEN

It has been said that bitterness is a cup of poison that we drink ourselves. Not only are our minds and spirits damaged by unforgiveness, even our bodies pay the price for the unhealthy stress it causes. Unforgiving people live in a state of continuous rage and spitefulness, and unfortunately experience little or no relief.

The closer we get to God on our quest, the more we become aware of how loving, patient, tolerant, and forgiving He is to us. The more we come to personally know His forgiveness, the more we can grant that same pardon to others. *God does not keep score.* Neither should we.

It is hard to hear from a God who is love and light when our minds are filled with hatred and darkness. Forgiveness is a step we need to make for our own health's sake. It takes that cup of bitterness out of our hands. But most important of all, it removes another barrier along our pathway toward God . . . and Ground Zero.

Relax.
Listen.
God is with you right here, right now.

Write your thoughts and responses to the following questions.

MORNING
Against whom are you holding bitter and unforgiving thoughts? Write down their names and their offenses.

MIDDAY
Make the conscious decision to forgive each person on your list. Tell God about each of the offenses, tell Him how it affected you, then ask His help in forgiving.

EVENING
Have you ever had to ask God or someone else for forgiveness? What happened? Have you forgiven yourself for the things you've done wrong in your life? If God has **forgiven** you, shouldn't you forgive yourself?

Journal of Days

WEEKEND

WEEK THREE: WHAT'S BLOCKING THE WAY?

DAYS NINE AND EIGHT

Overcoming the blockages and barriers that keep us from meeting God is one of the most important things we can do as we continue our journey toward Ground Zero. Not only is it important to us as far as our quest toward God is concerned, but removing those obstacles will change our relationships with others and with ourselves.

Once again, on this third weekend of your MindFast, I want you to seek out a solitary place, to cut off the cell phones, beepers, and other "leashes" that keep you attached to your everyday life. Quiet your mind, and seek quiet surroundings. Are you ready to hear what the "Big Guy" wants to say to you?

Relax.
Listen.
God is with you right here, right now.

BOTH MORNINGS
Spend time in complete solitude. Review your notes from the past week, and ask God to share His thoughts with you about what He may have been saying. Relax. Be still. Listen. Continue to let go of the things that have been blocking your way to God.

BOTH AFTERNOONS
As before, deliberately choose activities that are relaxing and as stress-free as possible. This week, also make an additional effort to release the barriers and blockages that may have kept you from listening to God. Breathe deeply. Concentrate on slowing down your pace. Give thanks for all the beautiful sights and sounds around you.

FIELD TRIP
Sit beside an open fire and write, on separate sheets of paper, each of the blockages that you have been struggling with this week. Write down each worry, each fear, each hurt, and whatever else you have been considering on separate pieces of notepaper. Take a moment to consciously release each concern, then throw the piece of paper in the fire and watch it burn.

Journal of Days

MONDAY

WEEK FOUR: WHO ARE YOU AND GOD TOGETHER?

DAY SEVEN

We never really get to know anyone until we invest some quality time in our relationship with them. Now that you have been spending time alone with God during your MindFast, you probably are beginning to recognize God's voice, to feel God's presence, and to realize that God is always with you. *Even when you aren't thinking about God, God is thinking about you.*

During this last week of our journey toward Ground Zero, we are going to focus on our partnership with God—who we are when God is with us. Who are you and God together? As we accept the reality that God is present in and around us, we are less afraid and more open with Him. We aren't expecting judgment, nor are we always begging Him for favors. Little by little, we are becoming aware of a genuine and mutual relationship with God who is truly there and who really, really loves us.

Relax.
Listen.
God is with you right here, right now.

Write your thoughts and responses to the following questions.

MORNING
Describe the changes you have experienced since you began to set aside time each day for your MindFast. What is keeping you from spending more time in solitude?

MIDDAY
What is your personal definition of *unconditional love?* Now that you've spent some time alone with God, are you seeing and feeling His unconditional love? Explain.

EVENING
If God is love, light, life, and the Creator of every living thing, how can He *not* be in everything, everywhere, and in everyone? Write your thoughts.

Journal of Days

TUESDAY

WEEK FOUR: WHO ARE YOU AND GOD TOGETHER?

DAY SIX

One day I asked Dee's seven-year-old daughter Mallory, "How does God talk to you?"

She smiled at me. "He just puts thoughts in your mind," she explained.

Once we have come to realize that God is love and light and life and that He loves us unconditionally, we begin to long to hear God's voice. Sometimes God speaks to us through nature, through music, through other people, through poems or other writings. But God also speaks to us through a still, small voice in our hearts and minds.

Hearing the voice of God usually requires silence, solitude, and a teachable spirit. But now and then it is so clear and so unmistakable that we could have heard it in the midst of a roaring crowd or a raging storm. We can make a point of seeking to hear God's voice, and in doing so, we can be sure of hearing it. Because God has promised that if we ask, we will receive, and if we seek, we will find. Doesn't it stand to reason, then, that if we listen, we will hear?

Relax.
Listen.
God is with you right here, right now.

Write your thoughts and responses to the following questions.

MORNING
God personally communicates with the men, women, and children of His creation. How can you recognize a thought that comes from God?

MIDDAY
Sometimes one particular person seems to stay in your thoughts. Why do you suppose that happens? What do you think you should do about it?

EVENING
When our mind slows down, relaxes, and withdraws from the constant noise and activity around us, we can receive thoughts and feelings that are unmistakably given by God. What are you thinking and feeling right now?

Journal of Days

WEDNESDAY

WEEK FOUR: WHO ARE YOU AND GOD TOGETHER?

DAY FIVE

As we experience the presence of God in our lives, His love begins to work through us, enabling us to care about all of creation, and especially about other people, some of whom we may never have even noticed before. God's love makes us comfortable enough with ourselves so that we can stop being self-centered and start being love-centered.

The wonder of living in the presence of God and having the presence of God living within us is that God's love, light, and Spirit become an integral part of our own nature. We find that we are changing from the inside out. We are hardly aware of the transformation, because it is God's work within us, which is made fully possible when we are at peace with the One who made us.

Relax.
Listen.
God is with you right here, right now.

Write your thoughts and responses to the following questions.

MORNING
How does knowing that you are unconditionally loved by God affect the way you relate to other people? List three people you could call today and thank or encourage or simply remind that you are thinking about them.

MIDDAY
Are you aware of people around you today who seem particularly sad, angry, or stressed? Say a prayer for them now and make a deliberate effort to share a kind word or smile with them later.

EVENING
How would you categorize the people with whom you have had personal encounters today? Lonely? Angry? Stressed? Happy? What do you think is keeping unhappy people from discovering God's love?

Journal of Days

THURSDAY

WEEK FOUR: WHO ARE YOU AND GOD TOGETHER?

DAY FOUR

God is the Creator of all things, and because we are made in God's image, we, too, are creative beings. We all have unique gifts and talents, and many of us haven't taken the time to develop them. Now that we have come to understand who we are with God in our lives, we begin to discover new interests, a new appreciation of beauty, and we begin to search for new opportunities to express our own creativity.

As we listen to God's voice and respond to the stirrings of God's presence within us, we will find awakening the special form of genius that is uniquely ours. With God's help, we can envision, imagine, form, shape, and produce one-of-a-kind creations—uniquely ours, but touched by the hand of the same God who fashioned the universe.

Relax.
Listen.
God is with you right here, right now.

Write your thoughts and responses to the following questions.

MORNING
Now that you are becoming aware of God's presence in your life, what would you most like to do in response to that presence? Is there something you have been afraid to try before?

MIDDAY
Have you ever created something on your own: a story, poem, painting, garden, woodwork, song, or some other project? Where did your inspiration come from? What part does God play in our creative ideas?

EVENING
Can you believe that your Creator has plans for you and Him to do some "creating" together? What do you think that means? What could you create with God as your partner?

Journal of Days

FRIDAY

WEEK FOUR: WHO ARE YOU AND GOD TOGETHER?

DAY THREE

One of the reasons we don't seem to experience God's presence in our lives is that we are either living in the past or fretting about the future. God is with us right here, right now. He is a God of the *present* tense. Are you living for today? I hope so, because that's where you'll find God, hear God, and experience God.

God is able to make the events of the past—even the most tragic and regrettable events—work out for the best. God is willing to lift the burden of the future off our backs and carry it for us, promising to manage it more wisely than we ever could. But God has given us one day, one hour, one minute to live at a time. In this very moment, He offers you Himself and all His power and presence could possibly mean to you. Are you willing to set aside "if only . . ." and "what if . . ." and receive God's gift of life today?

Relax.
Listen.
God is with you right here, right now.

Write your thoughts and responses to the following questions.

MORNING
Can you come to terms with the fact that God has been with you all your life, whether you were aware of His presence or not? Can you accept the reality that the sum total of your past, including His presence and activity in your life, makes up exactly who you are today?

MIDDAY
How do you deal with the fact that the future is unknown? How could your awareness of God's presence in your life change your emotions about the unknown future?

EVENING
Can you accept the "present" as a wonderful gift from God? List all the things you have to be thankful for today.

Journal of Days

WEEKEND

WEEK FOUR: WHO ARE YOU AND GOD TOGETHER?

DAYS TWO AND GROUND ZERO

This weekend marks the end of the beginning of your journey—your quest with God and toward God. You have thought deeply about who God is, who you are, and about the obstacles that have kept you from Him. And finally, you have begun to explore the possibilities of what life can be like when you acknowledge God's presence within you every moment of every day.

Please don't think, not even for a minute, that you've finished your quest. In fact, you've simply begun a life-long process of discovery and wonder. But I hope by now you've learned to value solitude, to appreciate nature, and to delight in the beautiful world around you. I also hope you've started thinking about what life could be if you lived it with a constant awareness of God's presence.

It's worth considering because God really is with you right now. God is listening to you, communicating with you, loving you, and hoping you'll catch a glimpse of His light, His love, His life, and His goodness. Are you listening? Are you starting to recognize His voice?

Relax.
Listen.
God is with you right here, right now.

BOTH MORNINGS

Spend time in complete solitude. Review your notes from the past four weeks, and ask God to share His thoughts with you about what He may have been saying. Relax. Be still. Listen.

BOTH AFTERNOONS

Once again, deliberately choose to relax and remain as stress-free as possible. If you can, for the next half-hour or so, turn off the cell phone and the beeper. Breathe deeply. Concentrate on slowing down your pace. Give thanks for everything beautiful you see around you.

FIELD TRIP

Today is your "present." Find a special, private getaway where you can freely talk to God as if He were physically sitting there with you. Then take a pad and paper and write a letter to Him, telling Him what your MindFast has taught you, how you'd like to *start all over again with Him* at Ground Zero. Write down any questions you still may have, and ask God, in His time, to provide the right answers. Then sign the letter, put it in an envelope, and open it a year from today. You'll be amazed to discover what God has done in your life!

A FINAL WORD

The book is finished, a Ground Zero weekend retreat has come and gone, and Dee, Tom, and I are back on my breezeway again. It's a lot quieter this time. There is more thinking, reflecting, and just being thankful than before. We three, though very different, have come to experience a "oneness" throughout this project. We have already decided that if the book doesn't sell ten copies and the whole experience was just for the three of us, individually and collectively, it was all worth it.

My thoughts keep drifting back to the faces of all the people I have talked to about God in the last four years. I keep seeing their eyes—people who I knew really wanted to know God personally and intimately. And no matter how much time I spend thinking about those faces, those eyes, and those conversations, I always flash back to that long-ago plane ride with Ken Stabler. His one simple question actually started all of this: "What do you think about the 'Big Guy'?" That same question, in one form or another, was asked of hundreds of people all over the country, and the compilation of their responses is our gift to you.

We are still, of course, the same three people—a creative, energetic mom and schoolteacher, an ex-hippie turned entrepreneur, and a sports/celebrity promoter. But, if it's even possible, we are more excited than ever about sharing our Ground Zero experiences. As we listen to the wind chimes singing in the breeze, I turn to Dee and Tom. "With all that we have experienced, heard, and seen, how would *you* answer Stabler's question—'What do you think about the "Big Guy"?'" Curiously, it was the first time we had asked each other how we would answer that question.

We grew even more quiet and thoughtful. Each of us envisioned a conversation with someone like Ken Stabler. It was Dee that broke the silence first: "I believe," Dee began, "that each of us is still a little child on the inside— a child that needs approval, needs acceptance, needs to know that he is loved just the way he is, warts and all.

"For me, God is the feeling of a soft lap, strong hands, and a gentle smile that says, 'I love you. I *delight* in you! I don't mean the "phony you" that you pass off to everyone else, but the *real you*. The you that nobody knows except you and Me.'"

Dee continued, "You see, God really is *crazy* about us. He cares so much about us that He squeezed Himself into an earth suit two thousand years ago so that nothing could stand between us and Him. He did that, knowing in advance every action we would ever take, every word that we would say, and every thought that would come into our minds. And He gave Himself to us anyway.

"God wants to be involved in everything that we do. He wants us to trust Him like a child who flings herself from the front porch into her father's arms. God will catch you when you jump. He's just waiting for you to jump so that He can prove His trustworthiness.

"Begin to look for Him everywhere. God will speak to you through the strength in a hawk's wings as it soars on the air currents, or in the delicate design of a snowflake or a butterfly wing, or in the colors of the sunset. God is in everything. Begin to look for His gifts and you will come to love and appreciate Him in a whole new way. You will feel His love and acceptance *personally*, and all you have to do to experience God's love for you is to jump into His arms."

Tom and I nodded our heads in agreement. We returned to our own thoughts for a few more minutes. Then Tom, with his own brand of theatrical flair, stood up and addressed an imaginary audience:

"There are people who will tell you exactly who God is and exactly what He wants you to do, especially where your time and money are concerned.

"Others will tell you to perform specific acts or to adopt a particular style or appearance in order to please God and receive His good favor. Some people, unfortunately, are so angry that their God can only be expressed as a curse word. Then there are those who will tell you that God is not involved in our lives at all or that He simply does not exist.

"Confusing isn't it? Welcome to Planet Earth circa A.D. 2000 But there is one thing I know for sure. God is waiting for you to take the first step. The entire universe is crying out for you to make up your mind. God's creation has a personal message for you if you will only be still and listen.

"Pascal wrote almost three hundred years ago, 'It is the heart which perceives God and not the reason. That is what Faith is: God perceived by the heart, not by the reason.'

"So take your heart to a quiet place and introduce yourself to God. Leave your intellect behind for just a few minutes and listen with your spirit. You'll learn more about God in one moment than I could tell you in a lifetime!"

As he took his seat again, he turned the tables on me and asked if my answer would be different now from what it was when Stabler asked the question the first time. I explained that my answer would probably be more in depth than it was four years ago, because my experience with Ground Zero has broadened my picture of God more than ever. By way of explanation, I shared with Dee and Tom some key points I've learned about God, points I gave to my son Marty the day he left for law school.

1. God is bigger than you have ever been told.*
2. God is more loving and tolerant than you have ever been told.

3. God is *crazy* about you!
4. God made you exactly the way you are for a reason.
5. God only wants good things for His kids.
6. There are no negatives in God.
7. God wants you to really *trust* Him.
8. There are no limits to God's love.
9. Anything you can imagine, anything your heart desires is yours—*if* you have the faith/trust to receive it and never doubt who is giving it to you.
10. Prayer is not just an exercise or preplanned ceremony. Prayer is exchanging thoughts with God—constantly!
11. God does not keep score.
12. No matter what you've done or how guilty you feel, God will always forgive you and welcome you with open arms.
13. The only thing that counts is really knowing the "Big Guy"!

And there it was—those were our answers, each very different in style, but the same in content. You might say that it was yet another example of how God reveals Himself through His people.

And now it is your turn. How would *you* answer that question? What do *you* think about the "Big Guy"? Is your answer different from what it would have been two years ago? Imagine you're talking with someone who keeps hammering you with probing questions: "Is

God real? What does God look like? What does God sound like?"

God, who is Spirit, became fully human so that we could hear, see, feel, and experience who God is, so that we could better understand the Father/Spirit that we can't see and touch. Through faith, we can now experience and hear the Father personally in our minds and hearts. In the biblical writings of John, Jesus describes for His best friends that God the Father is Spirit. He is light, love, life, truth, and peace, and Jesus declares that He is in fact God in human form. Jesus taught that everyone who earnestly desires to know the Father will experience the same oneness with God that He did.**

Nobody but you can discover your own answers and that will only happen if you know God personally and intimately. The "right" answer can't be provided *for* someone else or *by* someone else for you. It must come through personal experience. Only when you have personally encountered God can you stop knowing *about* God, and truly *know* God. And that, for us is Ground Zero:

Wondering about God
  Seeking God
    Discovering God
      Experiencing God
        Hearing and Seeing God
       Knowing God
        Loving God
          Starting all over again . . . with God.

*If you are interested in biblical references, following are texts that support the list of points I gave to my son (pp. 107, 108).

1. Psalms 139; 103:19; Isaiah 9:6
2. Psalm 103:8, 11; Matthew 11:28–29
3. Isaiah 46:3–4
4. Psalm 139:13–16
5. Psalm 103:5; 37:4
6. Psalms 23, 91
7. Proverbs 3:5–6; Matthew 6:25–34; Isaiah 26:3,4
8. Psalm 103:11–12; 1 John 4:8; Luke 15:11–32
9. Matthew 21:18–22; Psalm 37:4
10. Proverbs 2:1–6; Ephesians 3:14–21
11. Psalm 103:11–14; 1 Corinthians 13:4–5
12. Luke 15:11–32; 1 John 1:9
13. John 1:1–14; 17:3

**See John 1:1–14 and John 6:44–45.

For information on future MindFast™ Retreats or inquiries about speaking engagements for Ron Cook, Dee Kimbrell, or Tom Hicks, please call or write to:

Ground Zero™
P.O. Box 3007
Hendersonville, TN 37077
615/824-0886
or fax 615/824-0337